ONE MOMENT IN TIME

ONE MOMENT IN TIME

JILL PRIOR

APEX PUBLISHING LTD

First published in 2006 by
Apex Publishing Ltd
PO Box 7086, Clacton on Sea, Essex, CO15 5WN

www.apexpublishing.co.uk

Copyright © 2006 by Jill Prior
The author has asserted her moral rights

British Library Cataloguing-in-Publication Data
A catalogue record for this book
is available from the British Library

ISBN 1-904444-74-1

Typeset in 11.5pt Baskerville

Production Manager: Chris Cowlin

Cover Design: Andrew Macey

Printed and bound in Great Britain

For Stephen and Roger, my love and thanks for your constant support and not forgetting Lisa whose inspiration was always with me.

FOREWORD

Meeting Roger and Jill Prior in the summer of 1991 following the traumatic loss of their youngest daughter, Lisa, was to me no coincidence. To this very day, I think, no, I KNOW that this 'chance' meeting was arranged to perfection by their late daughter Lisa, in a desperate bid to help the Priors regain some sanity in a world that had now become so cruel to them.

I had been, in the early days of my mediumship, hungry to help others in their quest to find proof of survival of the spirit, and that is where the story begins - after one of my demonstrations one evening in 1991 came an open circle, but not before a welcome cup of tea was had by all.

Roger and Jill were introduced to me by Derek Telford, a medium whom I held in the highest regard and for whom I had the utmost respect. We chatted, for the most part, about general things - the weather and such like, and I suddenly got this sense that there was more to this introduction than met the eye. I said to both of them, "You know, both of you will be working in this spiritual field one day. I'm not sure how, but you will." And with that, and I will never forget it to this day, there was a blank look on Jill's face. It was as if I had just spoken in fluent Japanese! The palpable silence had an instantaneous way of making everyone else in the room aware to the fact that something had 'been said', and the atmosphere brought everyone to a halt. Roger looked a little wary, but that could be, looking back, Roger's way of dealing with Jill's very down to earth, 'feet stuck in a vat of concrete' look, which tends to embarass him somewhat! As I recall, Jill's reply was a little curt and to the point. "No, not us," she said, emphatically.

However, over the following few months, and to this day, both Jill and Roger have played an invaluable part in my life and, by their own admission, I have so in theirs, helping them in whatever small way I can to believe in the afterlife and the survival of the spirit.

This book will take you on a journey very different to most you have travelled, as it will emcompass a mother's loss of both a daughter and a best friend, and her seemingly 'unusual' way of coping with this grief - the dreadful pain and despair rising up again and again, and then moving on, with both Roger and Jill working through their own loss and at the same time helping others, using the precious knowledge that they have been so privileged to have found.

Needless to say, this book will take you on an emotional rollercoaster of tears, pain and sorrow, but also laughter; and yet, in the end, you can share Roger and Jill's happiness and security in the knowledge that their daughter Lisa did not die in vain. Through THEIR hard work, commitment and tireless efforts, Lisa has helped so many other people to understand and come to terms with the death of a loved one, more than anyone could imagine.

Finally, it will make you smile to know that, after all of this, Jill is STILL capable of giving you that withering look that makes you feel like a dandelion in the direct firing line of a squirt of weedkiller!

This, I'm sure you will appreciate, is an unusual quality in itself - to be involved in such a spiritual vibration, and yet to have your feet so firmly on the ground. For this, and many other qualities, Jill, we are grateful - grateful for your strength and compassion, but also for simply being the person you are today.

Most of all, we have got to thank Lisa, for without Lisa none of this would have been possible.

Stephen Holbrook, International Medium

INTRODUCTION

"Seek and you will find for you have aids from nature for the discovery of truth. But if you are not able yourself, by going along those ways to discover that which follows - listen to those that have made the enquiry" - **Epicetetus**

Each one of us in this life has a path that is chosen for us, some people may call it fate. But in February 1991 Roger and I were both unaware that 'fate' had chosen to alter our lives suddenly and drastically with no warning of what was about to happen. A single telephone call cut short our well ordered lives reducing us to a world of disbelief, horror and helplessness; it was the beginning of a long black tunnel that would stay with us for a long time.

This is the story of a beautiful young ballet dancer and teacher living happily in London, and how her path in life was suddenly and quite unexpectedly cut short at the age of 23 years. It describes the subsequent spiritual journey that Roger and I experienced over the last 15 years, and how we were fortunate to meet Stephen Holbrook a young medium with a wonderful gift of clairaudience a few months after Lisa died. The concept of eternal life, took on a new meaning when we listened to the proof that Stephen was able to give at his demonstrations. That our spirit never dies became a fact, and that no more did we have to rely on blind faith for the truth.

It also became obvious to us that many people experienced spiritual phenomena and for us in our quest for knowledge, it was necessary to delve further into the world of Spiritualism to enable us to have a more solid background for us to work from. We began to explore the history of religion and found out how it had gradually developed over the centuries into the many pathways, always initiated by man, so they could influence power and control over the people. All these pathways are supposed to lead to the eternal life of the soul or spirit, but sadly somehow the value and purpose of human life has been lost along the way on many of these paths, resulting in countless wars in the name of religion, causing much destruction and misery.

Since those early days we have met and listened to the testimonies of thousands of people who have been helped by Stephen's amazing compassion and love. He is able to give us all proof that indeed our loved ones are still around us and that we will all meet again. It is a privilege for Roger and I to be able to help with his demonstrations and to see how his gift has grown from strength to strength, in the fifteen years we have known him. Long may it continue to do so in the future.

In writing this book, I hope that the reader will realise that I am not a sad vulnerable mother desperately wanting a message at all costs! I am quite content to know that she is around us but for now I must get on with my life and travel the path that awaits me, because I know we will meet again some day.

CHAPTER 1

It was a Sunday morning in February, cold and with a sprinkling of snow that was certainly threatening to be a lot more than a mere covering. Our dogs needed their walk whatever the weather, so it was going to be a rushed breakfast and a quick walk over the fields, as Roger and I often attended the tiny Methodist church just at the top of our lane, and that Sunday morning was no different.

It was the beginning of half-term and our daughter Lisa was coming home on Tuesday to stay for a few days. She was teaching at the Central School of Ballet in London, but managed to come and visit whenever she had a few days to spare. While she was at home in the summer holidays she taught a small class of young children in the village hall, but because this break was only for a few days she would spend most of her time arranging class lessons and choreographing new dances.

Our two-bedroom cottage in a small Yorkshire village was perfect for Roger and me, as it was a reasonable size with a small garden. One of the bedrooms had recently been transformed into a makeshift office complete with a new computer and a desk - in addition to the single bed, wardrobe and dressing table for anyone who came to stay. Everything was a bit squashed, but nevertheless we managed somehow. Really it was Lisa's bedroom for when she came home. Roger worked from home for some of the time, but when Lisa came to stay she was given priority over the remaining space. Never the most tidy of people, her clothes and numerous ballet items would be strewn all over the room with the tape recorder taking priority on the dressing table - to play the many tapes required for practising her exercises. I looked forward to hearing her practise music, usually one of Chopin's études echoing around the house or possibly one of her favourite classical pieces that she loved to listen to - our house was filled with beautiful music whenever she came home. I made a mental note to put down the practice strip where she would exercise, as the constant scraping of her foot was wearing away the carpet! Her untidiness with her personal things was in complete contrast to what was required for her work schedule; she was very particular about her notes, and woe betide anyone who attempted to tidy away the odd scrap of paper, decorated with seemingly meaningless dance symbols, used for her choreography! The next few days (I mused) would be chaotic and enjoyable, but also demanding.

I was deep in thought when I was suddenly made aware that our two dogs, Paddy the Labrador and Rupert the Lurcher, were getting very restless. They were both eager to get on with their daily walk - and neither of them was in the mood to wait any longer! Lisa would enjoy taking over walking duties when she came home, as she loved to relax by walking miles over the beautiful moors near our home. I had given up joining her on these treks a long time ago, as she often strode ahead leaving me to catch up in my own time - I made excuses that my legs were shorter than hers, that I was a lot older and that I quickly got out of breath! Her superb fitness came from the early morning jogs around the streets in London where she lived, and also from swimming nearly every day - not forgetting the workouts she did for her ballet routines. Her energy put us to shame, and I wondered whether Roger would be persuaded again to join her on the early morning jogs over the next few days. Somehow I didn't think so.

I loved walking over the fields and through the woods with our dogs every day, as there was plenty of time to think and reminisce and to try to sort out any impending problems. Today was no exception; I was feeling elated at the prospect of Lisa coming home. It was always interesting to hear all her news of what was happening in the ballet school and what she had been doing since we last met. We had spoken often on the phone, but it was different when she came home - she brought the excitement of living in London back to Yorkshire. We were not just mother and daughter but also good friends and we enjoyed each other's company as we had a lot in common.

The last time I had paid a visit to see Lisa in London was in the previous November. I had been down to see her new accommodation in Stratford, east London. It belonged to Neil, a member of The Royal Ballet, whose father was the mystery voice behind Cilla Black's very popular *Blind Date* show. It was a nice house and the room she rented was a large bedroom - typically crammed with all her bits and pieces. Roger had been able to visit the house last month - he had to attend a business meeting in London, so it was an opportune moment for Lisa and Roger to meet up. They arranged to see the film *Ghost* and afterwards Lisa treated Roger to a curry in her favourite restaurant not far from her new abode. She was so pleased to have found this particular house, as accommodation was very hard to find in London and some of the rented rooms she had occupied previously left a lot to be desired. Still, beggars can't be choosers and so she made the most of wherever she stayed. Candles and flowers adorned her room, together with the odd bottle of red wine, which she always made sure there was plenty of, not only because she liked it herself but also to offer to anyone who came to visit!

When I had stayed with Lisa we had planned to do a tour of a few of her favourite haunts, and then on the Sunday before I was due to return home Lisa was going to show me around Kew Gardens. I was looking forward to that as it had been many years since my last visit and, being a keen gardener, I was excited to see how it had changed. However, a phone call from Roger on the Saturday morning had forced our plans to be put on hold. It had been snowing heavily in Yorkshire - roads were blocked and trains were being cancelled, so Roger was afraid that I wouldn't be able to return home as planned. Unfortunately at that time he was suffering from double vision, due to a virus, and relied on me to drive him to his appointments. Therefore getting back on time was a necessity. We were so disappointed at my having to return home earlier than planned, but Lisa understood my concerns and she insisted that I took her phone card with me in case the train was delayed. This was typical of her thoughtfulness and generosity. I hugged her goodbye and waved until she was out of sight. Never mind, I told myself, she would be home in February at half-term.

Lisa was the youngest of three girls. Her elder sister Frances was married with two children, Laura and Peter. Being auntie to them was something that Lisa loved, as she adored children, and she took every opportunity to visit them as they lived not far away in Derbyshire and often came over to visit whilst she was at home. Lesley was in the middle and the age gap between her and Lisa was only twenty-one months. She lived in the next village with her own daughter, Emma, and as she was so near Roger and I often called around to her tiny flat with bags of groceries. Lesley lived alone with her new baby and we constantly worried about how she was coping, but she insisted on managing by herself and didn't like us interfering - so our offers of help had to be very tactful. Lisa found it hard to get on with Lesley, because they both had such different personalities - often there were clashes when they met, and therefore Lisa chose not to seek out Lesley's company when she came home. Ah well, such is life - everyone is different and it would be a dull world if we were all the same! Somebody once told me that I should have had four children as the first and third pair off and the second and fourth pair off. I've often wondered if this were true. Apparently, with three, the middle one is always the one left out, but we had always tried hard to treat the girls as individuals and at the same time make sure that each was given the same opportunities.

I returned home from our walk with two wet but satisfied dogs, who waited patiently as I dried them off in the lobby. "Coffee?" asked Roger, as the welcome aroma of fresh coffee wafted from the kitchen. Walking over the fields - with a wind chill that seemed to take the temperature well below zero -was not one of the more pleasant duties in the morning. However, at least Paddy and Rupert were pleased with the outcome, and they would be happy for the rest of the day.

Frances phoned later in the morning to say that she wasn't too well, perhaps a touch of flu, and wouldn't be over to see Lisa that week. We caught up with each other's news and I mentioned that we might be able to pop over sometime when she was feeling a little better. The last thing Lisa would have wanted was to catch another virus, as it hadn't been long since she'd recovered from glandular fever. At least that is what the doctor said it was, but I was never convinced. The room she had been renting at that time was in Mornington Crescent. It was a tiny bedroom with a gas fire, comfortable enough but rather cramped, but still it was better than nothing. It wasn't a satisfactory place and I had an uneasy feeling about it when we had gone down to London to visit her. It had been a short time after she had moved in that Lisa phoned one day to say she was coming back home. She sounded terrible - hardly able to speak and saying that she felt ill - and, against our advice to stay in bed and call her doctor, she insisted on making the train journey back home. We met her at the station, and were shocked to see how ill she looked. As soon as we got back home we called our doctor, who came immediately; it was fortunate that he lived just down the road from us. He was amazed that Lisa had managed to make the journey back home being so ill, as she spent the next few days in hospital on a drip due to being so dehydrated. She came home from hospital and spent the next couple of weeks building up her strength, but within three weeks she had decided that she wanted to go back to London, against our advice and that of the doctor. Glandular fever had been mentioned but, looking back on her symptoms, I am not convinced it was that. There was no way that she could have returned to work so soon if it had been glandular fever, but she fretted and worried that she was neglecting her classes and no amount of arguing on our part could persuade her otherwise. So she went back to Mornington Crescent - Lisa was quite happy there, because not only was it somewhere to live but also it was near Camden market, which was her favourite shopping haunt. Her wardrobe was full of inexpensive pretty dresses bought from the stalls, which suited her tight budget. She was always careful with her money and saved as much as she could, but still made sure she always had enough to treat herself to nights out to the theatre or the cinema.

On the Monday morning we got up early - the dogs needed their walk and I needed to go shopping for the extra food as my cupboard was nearly bare. Because Lisa was a dancer with lots of energy, she had a healthy appetite, but she was also one of those lucky people who was naturally slim, even though chocolate was frequently on the menu! How I envied her, with her long arms and legs. She was so graceful in the way she moved, having a typical ballet dancer's physique. As a baby she was like a little doll and never suffered with puppy fat as she grew into her teens. Where she inherited her body from is a mystery, as her father, myself and her sisters are just the opposite.

I quickly prepared breakfast and Roger came down into the kitchen, saying that he had to go into the office that morning. We talked over what we were going to do that day when suddenly the phone rang. I answered it, wondering who on earth it could be so early in the morning. It was a call that would change our lives forever.

CHAPTER 2

"Mum, can I go to ballet classes?"

I groaned inwardly. "Oh, Lisa, surely you have enough to do with your riding and extra gym classes?"

What with being chauffeur to Frances and Lesley, with all their extra activities, the last thing we needed was another one added to the list! However, I was secretly quite pleased that Lisa wanted to start ballet, as I have always felt that it is beneficial to any young girl, helping with their posture and confidence. She was very good at gymnastics and her teacher had talked about her going in for competitions with a few of the others in her class. However, this was something that Lisa wasn't particularly bothered about and she had never pursued the idea, but she was still happy to attend extra classes after school. She had been blessed with a good brain and was top of her class in many subjects, never appearing to have to work too hard to achieve good results. Her end-of-term reports were outstanding and were always a credit to her; her teachers told us she was a child that had a lot of potential, whatever career choice she made.

If she wants to do ballet then perhaps something could be arranged locally, I thought - Roger's job took him out at odd hours and we were only a one-car family, so juggling our schedules was a constant battle. I would have loved a little 'runaround', but we couldn't afford another car at that time so it was no use idly wishing.

We lived in a village just outside Northampton at that time, and I had a part-time job in the local post office, so careful planning was required if we were to take on any more chauffeuring duties. I had been divorced with three children when I met Roger. We were both acting in a play at our local amateur theatre and, after several months of getting to know each other, we all moved in together! We married a few months later at Northampton Guildhall and the girls looked lovely as my bridesmaids. Our reception was held at the theatre in the village; it was an old barn that had been converted and stood in the large grounds of a house belonging to the local estate agent. It was a perfect day!

Later that evening I mentioned our conversation to Roger and we agreed that Lisa should only go for one term to see how she got on, as she was now eleven and we both thought her rather old to be starting ballet classes. There were no classes available in the village so it had to be in Northampton, and due to Lisa's persistence we found a class run by Mollie Mayhew on Saturday mornings. Making further enquiries, we found it had a good reputation. Frances was working in the local open-air market for extra pocket money on Saturdays and had to be there conveniently a bit earlier than the start of Lisa's dancing class. Lesley was quite happy to stay at the stables with her beloved horses, whose company she preferred, or visit her father who lived not too far away from us. She certainly wasn't interested in ballet classes!

Lisa was allowed to start at the dancing school in the middle of the term, so the following Saturday we all set off for what was set to become a regular routine. Having left Frances at the vegetable stall, we walked along the road to the hall with Lisa clutching her new ballet shoes with a good deal of excitement and anticipation. As we entered the front door we were greeted by the sound of excited chattering coming from the cloakroom. The smell of leather from the ballet shoes pervaded the air, mingling with the dusty odour of an old church hall. We found mums, some trying to persuade tights onto legs that wouldn't stay still, and some with leotards and ballet shoes spilling over onto the floor from open bags; there was an air of frenzy. Lisa and I joined the mêlée and Roger stood tactfully outside while everyone was changing. It seemed there were dozens of tiny tots milling around, all wanting their hair brushed and drawn back with the regulation pink hairband so that no strand of hair was out of place. There was the sound of a cane rapping on the dance floor and a voice shouted, "Hurry up, please!", followed suddenly by an almighty rush towards the door to the studio. A tinny old piano came to life and all the little ones were at once quiet and orderly, and there was our Lisa standing tall amongst them all, not in the least bit bothered that she was quite conspicuous. Miss Mayhew, with stick in hand, walked around each child correcting their posture with a gentle prod. We wondered again how long Lisa's enthusiasm would last, but she calmly joined in and concentrated on her 'good toes and naughty toes', not looking back at us as we departed to find a coffee shop to while away the time. Those Saturday morning classes fuelled the beginning of her love of ballet, as well as classical music, and after that first trial term it became her life and passion.

Any parent that has become involved in their children's passions will know the dedication, time and, of course, cost that are necessary to help them succeed; so it was for us. Frances was busy with her GCEs. She was sixteen, wanted to be a nurse, and had her own circle of friends and a boyfriend - an interest in ballet was not on her agenda. She was studying hard to obtain the necessary qualifications for a career in nursing, as she had been accepted at our local hospital. Lesley's passion was working in the local stables and, having decided that she wanted a career working with horses, she had no time for her younger sister's new-found interest either. Consequently, over the next few years Roger and I would find our lives ordered to fit in with the children, a problem that I am sure is familiar to many parents!

Because Lisa started ballet later in her young life, there was a lot of catching up to do with the rest of her class - the majority of children were around the age of four and some had started from as young as two! It was obvious from being able to watch the classes that some of the children had a natural ability and thrived in the atmosphere of the class. Others were there simply because they were told it would be good for them and not because they had a particular desire to dance. Lisa was there because she was sure it was what she wanted to do and it seemed to us, as we watched her in the classes, that she did have both a natural grace and the right build for ballet. With all three girls, we encouraged them to make their own choices in what paths they wanted to pursue rather than follow what we wanted, because we believed that if you are happy in what you are doing then achievement will come naturally.

Lisa's school was quite sympathetic to her career choice, although when it came to taking her GCEs they insisted she took up typing, which she hated, but it was "just in case things don't work out for you" her teachers told her, and she also had to give up gymnastics as it used muscles that weren't good for ballet!

Our regulated life took a sudden change when Roger's work required us to move to Yorkshire. Finding a house and another ballet school took priority and after several journeys up to Yorkshire we finally found both. Frances, who had started her orthopaedic hospital training and was now happy living in the nurses' home, would be staying in Northampton to complete her course and she then had plans to do her general nursing; she was independent and content with her choice of career.

After settling into our new house in a lovely area called Denby Dale, Lesley and Lisa enrolled at their school, and we found a ballet school in Brighouse with a very good reputation where, for the next three years, Lisa worked extremely hard to catch up with her fellow dancers. She had a wonderful teacher whose passion for dance enthused her pupils, all of whom adored her. Some of the pupils in Lisa's class had already been to London to audition for places at the Royal Ballet School and were awaiting their results - there was an air of excitement and anticipation in the school. It didn't take long before Lisa's teacher realised that here was another potential candidate for a 'proper' ballet school and so the hard work towards her dream started. She became centred on attaining her goal, so much so that socialising with her school friends was limited and boyfriends and parties were unheard of. London beckoned.

Exams were taken and she passed well, mostly with honours, and we made the obligatory trips to shows and competitions - I was amazed at how many mothers were living their dreams through their children and how over-zealous some of them were. Welcome to the competitive world of ballet!

I had to learn quickly how to darn the ballet shoes and sew on the ribbons, attach hundreds of sequins on the costumes required for the shows and arrange her hair in a net with all the hairpins so that not a strand was out of place, but most importantly I had to be available for chauffeuring!

Lisa's teacher decided that she should apply to a couple of ballet schools: The Central School of Ballet in London, and the Doreen Bird College outside London. The Central was founded by Christopher and Carol Gable, both Royal Ballet members, and it had achieved an international reputation for being one of the top ballet schools in London and this one was Lisa's first choice.

Lisa was accepted by Doreen Bird, but all she wanted to do was ballet and she decided to await the outcome of her audition at the Central. In the meantime, Roger and I approached the council and applied for a grant towards the cost of lodgings and school fees. There was no way that we would ourselves be able to afford the tremendous costs involved and we hoped desperately that Lisa would qualify for a grant. After much form filling and interviews we sat back and waited.

Two long weeks later it was confirmed that Lisa had been successful at the Central. We were so happy for her, but the reality of the situation hit us when we received a long list of all the items she required for her dancing and we also had to find lodgings for her near the ballet school. A letter also arrived a few days later from the council saying that we had been successful in our application and Lisa was awarded a full grant for her lodgings and ballet school fees. We asked for help from other parents who were more 'in the know' than us and had been in the same situation. We knew it wasn't going to be easy because so many students were looking for somewhere to stay, and living in Yorkshire meant several journeys down to London, which we found rather daunting. It was also the time of the London bombings by the IRA, but when we mentioned our concerns to Lisa she brushed them aside saying that she would be all right but too bad if she was in the wrong place at the wrong time. Such was her desire to go to London that everything else was of little importance - it was left to Roger and me to do all the worrying!

The first place we tried was a large respectable-looking house run by nuns, which had been recommended to us by other parents as being ideal as a 'starter home'. On knocking, a large nun in an equally large black cloak opened the door to welcome us in to look around. It was very sombre and to some extent rather austere, but there were other ballet dancers staying there so it couldn't be that bad, could it? We decided that it was at least a safe place and perhaps a good choice for Lisa seeing as she was a stranger in London and not used to busy town life. We felt secure in the thought that Lisa was with others who shared the same interests and that the nuns would look after her, but as I was saying goodbye to my youngest and last child to leave home, I felt empty and tearful on our journey home to Yorkshire.

The first phone call from Lisa came not long after she had moved in, and I cannot repeat some of the stories she told us. The food rations were on a starvation level for the dancers, while on the nun's table situated in full view of everyone else the food was infinitely more desirable. Then there were complaints about the tiny bedroom. It was so small that there wasn't enough room for two people and all the clothes that they were required to have - and the nuns obviously had their favourite boarders! Lisa was clearly very unhappy there, so in desperation she tried again to find different accommodation. This was when she found a room in Mornington Crescent, and we made the journey down to London to inspect her new premises. It was in a rabbit warren of a house with lots of little staircases and dozens of doors leading to dozens of rooms - one had to memorise the way back to Lisa's bedroom, which was at the top of the house! Although providing enough room for the essentials, it wasn't particularly inviting, but with her usual few candles and flowers and a handful of personal possessions it became Lisa's home for the next couple of years.

We loved going down to the Central to see the end-of-term productions, and to witness the progress Lisa had made. I loved the special atmosphere of the school, seeing the dancers in their classes working so hard at the barre, together with the sound of the beautiful ballet music echoing all over the building. Every young person there was fulfilling their dream and no amount of blood, sweat and tears could make them think that it wasn't worth it. Sometimes I was coerced into darning Lisa's ballet shoes, a job she used to hate - I was the one who ended up with sore and pricked fingers, trying desperately not to soil the pink satin with spots of blood! This is a job every dancer has to do with new shoes, to stop the points wearing away too soon, and usually more than one pair of shoes is needed - it was a job I never got used to and neither did Lisa. Sometimes, while waiting for her to finish her class, we were permitted to watch Christopher teaching the young boys. I shall never forget the sweat streaming down their faces as they completed their exercises with hardly a pause for breath! Anyone who thinks that ballet is for 'sissies' doesn't know what they are talking about.

We received reports on Lisa's progress throughout the year and were told of any injuries she sustained. They were usually minor strains and nothing to worry about. In her second year we were told her back was giving her some trouble and they had arranged for a Harley Street specialist to have a look. Because she had had to miss some classes, she felt she still had to practise and exercise to keep up; however, she didn't realise at the time that she was damaging her back even more. It was a few months later that we received a phone call to say that pupils were being interviewed by the staff who would then give an assessment of how they were progressing and, as Lisa was one of them, would I please make sure that I attended the interview with her. I thought this seemed rather a strange request, so I asked a few more pertinent questions. It transpired that Lisa was not going to be allowed to continue at the school through to the next year, as any more strain on her back could cause irreversible damage, and they had not yet told her.

That train journey was the worst of my life. All I could think of was how Lisa was going to take the news; her dream was about to be shattered. It was quite common, I was told, for some girls to feel suicidal and that is why they wanted me to be with Lisa. Roger was unable to go down with me and I wanted his company so much at this awful time.

I walked into the school with trepidation, and as soon as Lisa saw me she knew it was going to be bad news. I will never forget that interview. With tears streaming, she pleaded and pleaded to be given another chance, saying she would try harder and that she really would be all right. But all the staff were adamant that she would injure her back too severely and they were not going to let that happen; it was too great a risk. There was nothing I could say to them; they were the experts and they knew what was best, but what comfort could I give Lisa? She was sobbing her heart out and wouldn't listen to me or anyone else. Then suddenly Carol said that if Lisa would consider a career in teaching ballet she would be delighted to have her back at the Central as a teacher. A lifeline had been thrown, but Lisa was too distressed to take it in. However, I was so grateful and relieved, as it would give us all something to think about. In my mind there was a light, after all, at the end of a very dark tunnel.

The next few weeks were such a difficult time. Emotionally, Lisa was drained and she refused to see the lifeline that Carol had thrown her. We tried to talk to her but it was no use, she wouldn't listen - as far as she was concerned her world had fallen apart.

Eventually, after a couple of months and after much talking and gentle persuasion, she agreed at least to look at the possibilities of becoming a ballet teacher. The London College of Dance in Bedford agreed to see Lisa, and after several interviews the principal suggested she join the second year given her time at the Central School in London. It was so different to a ballet school - the girls were all different shapes and sizes, not like the consistently stick thin girls at the Central - and Lisa found it very hard to adjust. I told her that if she wanted to stay within the ballet world she should take what the College had to offer and make it work for her. She accepted that she could no longer dance, but if she were able to teach she would still be surrounded by the ballet world, so perhaps there was a light at the end of the tunnel.

She moved down to Bedford, and at least this time it was easier to find decent accommodation and Lisa at long last began to realise the potential she could achieve as a teacher, especially if she eventually joined the staff at The Central. During the next couple of years she worked hard for the exams to qualify as a dance teacher, gaining honours. She even won a bursary, awarded for excellence in ballet, and this enabled her to travel to Budapest to see some of the ballet schools at work there. Travelling to London one day each week, she studied the Cecchetti ballet method to enable her to teach it and passed her exams with honours. To maintain her fitness she went swimming early every morning, arriving at College well before anyone else, as well as attending her usual exercise classes. The college productions were held in the nearby theatre and it became evident that she had a flair for choreography and she was chosen to choreograph a dance entitled 'The Life of Helen Keller' - Lisa danced the part of the blind and deaf Helen, and her close friend, Ali, danced the part of her teacher. It was emotionally a very moving piece of choreography, and the staff of the College were so impressed with her work that they created an award especially for her. We were so proud of her and the way she had turned things around to enable her to carry on with her love of ballet.

Much to our surprise, Lisa was chosen for the cover of the college brochure to advertise their ballet classes. I say 'surprise' as Lisa never mentioned it to us and it was quite by chance that we happened to see it when the college sent us a copy! That was typical of Lisa - she was very reserved about her successes and information had to be prised out of her. Once, when Roger and I congratulated her on a very successful exam result, she brushed it off as if it were nothing much and she could have done better. This was Lisa the perfectionist; she would never push herself forward but preferred to gain recognition by the results of her hard work.

We attended the diploma ceremony at the end of her course together with her grandparents who had travelled all the way from Somerset. It was a very emotional occasion for us all. After the traumatic times Lisa had been through over the previous few years, she was now looking forward to going back to the place she loved, to teach and help the younger ones to live their dreams.

Carol and Christopher welcomed Lisa back, and joining their staff made Lisa feel that she was back where she belonged. Once again she moved to London having found a room in a house in Stratford. At last she was settled in her work and very happy to be teaching the 'little ones' who adored her - and she was renting a room in a 'decent' house. Life was on the 'up' once more. Holidays were spent in Yorkshire and, as it was half-term in the next couple of days, she would be going home for another well-earned rest.

CHAPTER 3

At first the voice on the telephone made no sense; I hadn't heard properly. It was my ex-husband John saying that Lisa had had an accident.

"What's happened to her? Is she hurt?" I started to panic - she was coming home tomorrow.

John asked if anyone was with me and suggested that I sit down. He could hardly speak and there were long silences.

"What's the matter?" I kept repeating, getting impatient.

John was the father of our three children, and we had been through a painful divorce many years previously when the girls were much younger. He never had much to do with the children, and if he were honest he should never have married, as he would have preferred to have stayed a bachelor. We hadn't been in contact for some time, but here he was on the telephone telling me to sit down!

"Lisa's dead."

He repeated the words. He wasn't making sense. I remember screaming "No, no!" Roger came over and took the phone from me. He remembers thinking, who is this Lisa that John is talking about? Certainly not our Lisa who is fit, strong and healthy. The conversation was just as surreal to him as to me. I cannot describe what went through us. The emotion is too powerful to put into words - a combination of fear, disbelief and horror. Roger and I clung together and we both sobbed - such a feeling of helplessness, we didn't know what to do next; we felt lost.

Lisa was in London, so far away. We hadn't been there for her, and she had died alone.

If I am honest, writing this now, I feel sick at the memory so I will just explain the circumstances that had occurred as we learnt them over the next few hours.

Our beautiful, lovely Lisa had gone into the bathroom early on the Sunday morning as usual and had been overcome by carbon monoxide fumes from the boiler that was situated in a nearby cupboard. It had been snowing in London the previous night and the outside flue had become blocked, meaning that the fumes had nowhere to go except into the bathroom. She had breathed in all those deadly fumes without realising it - carbon monoxide is a silent killer; you cannot see it or smell it. Lisa had died in minutes, and at the house in which she was so happy to be living - how ironic!

One thing I will explain to you readers is that, in spite of Lisa's thoroughness as regards her work, she had not put in her filofax our telephone number and address as next of kin - she probably thought she didn't need to write them down, as she knew them off by heart - and therefore the police were unable to inform us on the Sunday morning. Through their enquiries from the addresses she had written down, they managed to trace her father who went down to London to identify her body. He then called us on the Monday morning.

The devastating news was broken to her sisters and then to the rest of the family. Everyone was in a state of total disbelief. The following days and weeks remain a horrible blur with vague memories of the doctor calling to see if I required any pills. Because I was letting all my grief come out, he thought I wouldn't need any, and he assured us that Lisa would have just fallen asleep and wouldn't have suffered, if that was some comfort. Friends and neighbours were coming around at various times, helping with mundane tasks that I found I wasn't able to do due to lack of concentration, and James our minister was there for us to offer pastoral comfort. Roger and I were supporting each other but lurching from pillar to post, not sleeping, weeping and just being on autopilot. I kept on saying, to whoever would listen, that I wanted Lisa back home - the longing to see her once more was so great. Eventually, after all the formalities, she was brought back home to Yorkshire and laid in the chapel of rest. Roger and I went to see her the following day and I remember thanking God that, outwardly, her beautiful body had been unharmed. She looked so delicate and, as I held her hand and stroked her hair, I remembered how she had said, when I worried about her living in London with the IRA bombs going off, that, "If I'm in the wrong place at the wrong time so be it." Oh Lisa, you *were* in the wrong place at the wrong time, I cried inwardly, but I had to be strong for everyone; I didn't want to break down in front of them. As we said goodbye, we put a Valentine card in her hand, which had been waiting for her at home - to this day I don't know who it was from.

Grief is such a personal thing; everyone can react differently. Although books have been written with the intention of making people aware of the gamut of emotions that one can experience, how one person reacts to the same situation can be entirely different to another's. Lisa's sisters were completely the opposite to each other in dealing with their grief. Frances wanted to say her goodbyes to Lisa, and she and Michael took Laura, who was four, in with them, having carefully explained that Auntie Lisa had gone to heaven and they were going to say goodbye to her. Laura placed her teddy bear in the coffin and said that Auntie Lisa looked like Sleeping Beauty. Lesley, on the other hand, didn't want to see Lisa at first and it was only on persuasion that she reluctantly went to say goodbye. She has never forgiven us for persuading her and was never able to discuss her thoughts, remaining private and silent. She grieved inwardly, not wanting to unburden herself or share her grief, and she pushed away all offers of help from the family. It is sad that the anger within her has never been resolved in the passing years.

The day of the funeral came. It is a jumble of memories to me now, having been deliberately pushed to the back of my mind. I can remember the hearse standing outside the cottage laden with flowers and the whole scene being surreal to Roger and me. Following the hearse in the car behind, we set off for the church which was situated up a steep hill from where we lived. Suddenly Lisa's coffin started swaying violently and the flowers were bumping around, threatening to fall off. The cars stopped. We all looked at one another and started to giggle. I am sure it was a spontaneous nervous reaction, but Lisa would have done the same thing. We said that she was having the last laugh and it would be typical of her sense of humour - a wicked one! Looking back, I think she was trying to stop us from being too miserable and solemn. We were told that it was the first time it had ever occurred, the hearse having suddenly got a puncture. It had been fine for the journey to our cottage, it was a mystery, but it would be repaired as soon as we arrived at the church, the man in charge said - that is if it made it up the steep hill, I thought. We made an extra slow journey to the top of the hill, and with a sigh of relief we arrived safely.

The church was full of friends and relatives. Staff from the Central School of Ballet and Bedford College attended, to speak glowingly of her achievements. Roger and I had chosen a piece of music that was to be played during the service - 'Claire du Lune' - one of the very first piano pieces she had danced to in a competition. As it was playing I couldn't help myself and just wept with everybody else, but we felt so proud of what she had done in her short life - she had lived it 200% - and now that life had ended so abruptly.

She was buried in the cemetery a short walk away from the cottage, and in the spring we planted purple primulas all around her grave. The stone was chosen from the local quarry and we had permission from the Church Council to have a pair of ballet shoes engraved above the words:

A ballet dancer and teacher
Whose grace and love
Inspired and touched
The hearts of so many
'She will always be with us'

CHAPTER 4

Trying somehow to instil a normal routine into the days ahead was impossibly hard. We couldn't concentrate and both of us found it difficult to sleep. Sometimes I would get up in the early hours, go down to the kitchen and cry silently just thinking jumbled thoughts and asking myself what on earth was the point of life. Roger often joined me as he too was lying awake unable to asleep, and we would talk and cry together and remember the times we had with Lisa. Roger was neglecting his work but had no enthusiasm for it, and reluctantly he made the gesture of an appearance in the office but his heart wasn't in it and he spoke a lot about leaving. Sometimes James, our minister, would pop in for a coffee in the morning and we ended up having intense discussions - has Lisa really gone to heaven? How can we be sure? I know we are promised these things in the Bible, but how does anyone know for certain what is ahead of us? There isn't any proof of a heaven, but this is what we wanted from James - a certainty that there is everlasting life and that Lisa had gone to heaven, wherever that was. After all, this was what we had been brought up to believe. With all the work and trauma one has to go through just to achieve survival in this life, what is the point if there is nothing at the end of it? But if there is, how can we be sure there is? This question just kept going over and over in our heads.

The days passed in a blur. I felt tired and sick with grief and Roger wasn't settling at work and was in the middle of 'looking around'. We didn't recognise that we were not capable of making rational decisions, and Lisa's death only heightened the unsettled feelings that we both had. Roger's grief was as great as mine and, even though Lisa was not his own daughter, the love and respect he had for her, since meeting her as a seven year old, were very strong. He had been an 'older brother' and confidant who was always there for her, and he had shared her wicked sense of humour - making their bond as strong as any father and daughter. I found solace in walking with the dogs and just sitting in the woods talking to and thinking about Lisa. I still couldn't believe she had gone and one of the easiest things for me to do was to imagine that she was on holiday abroad somewhere and couldn't get to the phone. I also imagined her voice saying, "Hi mum", which was how she started her phone calls and I could hear her asking, "You all right?" Where are you Lisa? I thought.

Friends and neighbours would call and I would talk about Lisa. I couldn't stop myself. They would patiently listen while I rambled on, and to this day I thank them for their understanding and patience. I couldn't listen to any ballet music on the radio; in fact I couldn't listen to any music at all, as tears were all too near the surface and it didn't take much to evoke memories. Frances would phone and we would spend so long comforting each other with words of advice on how to get through the days to follow. Lesley occasionally came to visit but studiously avoided any talk of Lisa, and we would skirt around the subject of how she was coping with Lisa's death, instead concentrating on how Emma her daughter was progressing and talking about all the trivia of normal everyday life.

Roger and I would often take the short walk to visit her garden - I have never liked calling it her grave - and we would stand there alone in our thoughts. It didn't seem possible that she was buried there, but I felt nearer to her as I tended her garden.

There were terrible days when I would just sit in her room, gather one of her dresses in my hands and just try to smell the familiar scent to bring her a bit closer again. The pain was so great that I wondered how I could continue each day - there just didn't seem any point any more. Even though I still had family around me, I was wrapped up in my own thoughts and my pain just shut out everything else. I knew that Lesley didn't like coming over to see us as she found it too difficult to face our hurt and cope with hers as well.

Frances decided to cope with her raw emotions by unburdening her anger at what had happened. These are her words:

"On the morning of the call from Mum telling me that Lisa was dead, I was at home feeling unwell. I didn't know it then, but I was about to go down with a bad bout of flu. I rang Mike at work; I can't remember what I said to him, but he came home straight away. I don't think I cried at that point as I was in a state of shock. I had this overwhelming need to be near Mum, so we just got into the car and drove over to her house. I felt numb inside and just couldn't take in what had happened. It was over the next few days that the grief really set in. I think the key point for me was that I was able to talk to Mum about my feelings - if it wasn't for her I don't think I would have got through it."

I mentioned about the different feelings of grief because they are emotions that can have a lasting effect on the way we cope with our lives. Grief has no set pattern and doesn't have a time limit. There is a saying that time heals, but it doesn't; what it does is to help one to cope with the wounds that will always be there. I feel it is necessary for anyone who is grieving to be able to have an outlet for their grief and to be able to talk with someone who will listen. This is why the bereavement counsellors are there for you if you have no one in your family you can turn to. Frances has been able to come to terms with the loss of her sister, but in contrast Lesley has found it more difficult to be open about it and talk with us even some years later.

Several months had passed when Lesley casually mentioned that we ought to go to a Spiritualist church, as her neighbour often went and we might possibly find some comfort for ourselves. We were rather taken aback at her suggestion as this was something totally alien to us, having been brought up in the socially acceptable religion of our respective families. After all, wasn't Spiritualism rather spooky and about talking to the dead, and therefore taboo in many circles? However, it was a thought that kept nagging at us and, as we were both open minded and following several discreet enquiries with Lesley's neighbour, we plucked up the courage to go along on a Sunday evening a few weeks later. We didn't know what to expect but I did wonder if a Spiritualist meeting was on similar lines to a Quaker meeting.

The service was being held in an old church hall in a little village not too far away. We parked the car, noticing with relief that there were quite a few cars already there - surely that was a good sign, I thought. It was with a good deal of trepidation that we entered the hall to be welcomed by a couple who were handing out hymn books. The chairs were arranged in a semicircle in rows, not like the traditional pews in a church, and quite a lot were already occupied. People were laughing and chatting together, making the atmosphere friendly, and we sat down feeling a bit more relaxed - only a bit, mind you, as I still felt rather nervous not knowing what to expect. Looking around at the people seated, it was noticeable that many had come along without necessarily putting on their 'Sunday best', especially the young ones. Anyone and everyone was there - what a difference to how it usually is in our church where it seemed to be far more formal, I was thinking.

The service was presided over by the lady who ran the church. Her name was Una, we learnt later, and she was so friendly in her manner that we warmed to her instantly. There were new hymns that we sang, and the prayers were what I would call down to earth and understandable! There was a healing list of names of those who were ill and needed our thoughts, and this was read out by Una. We particularly liked this as it made it more personal to us, and this was followed by a demonstration of mediumship given by a lady who was known as 'the singing bus conductress'. We hadn't ever seen a medium at work before and didn't know what to expect. I can tell you all now that it left us feeling completely bemused and with a 'what on earth was that all about?' attitude to it. All she did was sing every other sentence and walk up and down the hall, pausing just long enough to convey a message before breaking into song again! Roger and I tried to stifle our giggles and we can only thank goodness that Lisa wasn't physically there with us as we would not have been able to control ourselves - I just hope that nobody noticed the ignorant newcomers. I'm afraid that that part of the evening meant very little to us, in fact we thought it very strange, but we did like the service, especially the spontaneity of the prayers and the healing list.

Afterwards we introduced ourselves to Una. We explained that we were new and had never been to a Spiritualist service before, and that it had been suggested to us that we come along because we had recently lost our daughter. She was kindness itself and introduced us to some of the other mediums, who were only too pleased to talk about their gift, and they reassured us that our Lisa was well and happy. At this point we felt too overwhelmed by what they were saying to take anything in properly, but as we had both enjoyed the service we decided to go again the following week. Perhaps we were also clinging on to some hope that Lisa was still around us and that she hadn't left us for ever.

The following week we arrived at the 'church' and felt a bit more at ease. We were surprised at the number of people attending, as it always seemed to be full. Again the hymns had me in tears, and after the service we chatted with another member of the congregation who, noticing how upset I was, mentioned that we should meet this young lad who had a lovely gift of mediumship. He led us over to a small group of people gathered in a corner and called out, "Stephen, come and meet Roger and Jill. They have just lost their daughter." A young man turned around and greeted us with a warm smile. With his long blond hair tied back in a ponytail and his designer stubble with hooped silver earrings, he appeared to us the most unlikely person to give us any comfort in our situation! But there was something about him that we instantly liked. Don't ask me what as I don't know; maybe it was his unassuming manner or his concerned look when we explained to him about Lisa. Whatever it was that drew us to him, we chatted for a long time. We didn't know it then, but this was the start of something extraordinary for both of us and something that would change the rest of our lives forever.

CHAPTER 5

"You are going to be working in this one day," said Steve.

I spluttered. "Not likely," I mumbled.

Roger was rather amused - he knew that I was very 'grounded', and very sceptical about anything that was yet to be explained or proven.

"You are," Steve continued, "just you wait and see. By the way, have you done anything with a large picture of your daughter recently?"

"No," I replied instantly.

But Roger's reaction took me by surprise. "Yes you have, you moved that one of her looking rather haughty, in her black tutu, back into her room, as it made you think she was following every move we made in our bedroom!"

"Oh, that one!" I exclaimed. "Yes, I felt she was looking down at us, so I moved it into her bedroom," I explained hastily. I felt awkward, perhaps a bit embarrassed that someone should be telling me what I had done with Lisa's picture, but she really does have this haughty look on her face that seems to follow you wherever you are!

Stephen was so interesting to listen to that we hadn't realised most people had already gone home, and he really did seem very interested in us! When we said our goodbyes and thanked Stephen we asked whether we would perhaps see him again soon.

"Yes, I shall be working in next week's service," he replied.

We had found it so comforting to hear everyone at the hall

talking about those that they had lost being around them still, and we just hoped that the same was true for Lisa.

I had been chatting to a medium earlier, before the service, and he had asked me, "Have you felt Lisa around you?"

"No, not at all," I had replied. I explained that both of us spoke to Lisa as if she was with us, but I felt nothing of her presence and neither did Roger.

"When you go to bed you don't feel her hand in yours?" he asked.

"No, nothing," I had responded, feeling slightly irritated by now. It was all right for him - he was sensitive as they call it, able to feel and sense spirits around him - but here he was asking someone who had never had anything happen that could be called even slightly out of the ordinary! I found it very difficult even to imagine what it would be like to experience anything unusual - would I be excited and accept it or would I just brush it off with my usual scepticism?

We hadn't mentioned to Frances or to any other member of the family that we had been attending a Spiritualist church for the past couple of weeks, maybe because we still felt awkward about the whole concept of 'spirits' and 'talking to the dead' and 'mediums'. It was still very strange and alien to us and, besides, we felt that we wanted to find out more on our own and not be influenced by anyone else's point of view.

We decided to make an appointment to visit Una to see if she could help us answer some questions. She was very happy to help us in any way she could, being a medium herself, and invited us over the following week. Sadly her husband was not well and our time with her was very short.

However, she agreed to give us a 'reading' to see if Lisa would come through. As has already been mentioned, I am very grounded and do not feel, hear or sense anything at all spiritually, and Una's reading didn't really touch anything special for me. However, Roger gained more from it and says he has never forgotten those first words from Una. In Roger's own words: "The first thing that Una said to us was, 'Why am I seeing flowers swaying from side to side?' Her hands were swaying from left to right, rather like a pair of windscreen wipers." To Roger that was an amazing thing to come straight out with, as she had no knowledge of the puncture in the tyre of the funeral car, resulting in the flowers swaying from side to side. Yes, I must admit that did seem strange that Una had actually spoken about the flowers, but then I think my expectations were too high and that Lisa would come through more directly, so my response to the reading was more on the negative side.

Una had founded the Spiritualist church with her husband some years before, but now that he was ill she was carrying on alone. She is a very well-respected medium and she and Steve have done a tremendous amount for charity. It was she, together with others, who helped Steve in the earlier days to gain the confidence to start his public demonstrations. I just wish that, at the time I had the reading from Una, I had known a bit more about Spiritualism, as I might have appreciated it a bit more.

We eventually told Frances about attending the Spiritualist church and, far from being horrified at the idea, she and Mike were quite interested. It was in passing that she mentioned about a lifelike dream that she had had, two days after Lisa's death. Again, I quote her own words:

"Two days after Lisa's death I dreamt that I met Lisa on a bridge. It was a sunny day and we appeared to be in the countryside. She said to me, 'I know I'm not alive, but I don't feel as if I'm dead. Please find out what happened to me.' I promised that I would. I then asked if I could touch her hand and she said, 'Yes.' I touched her hand and I remember how surprised I was that it felt so soft and warm. It was at that point that I woke up sobbing."

"Have you dreamt about Lisa?" she asked.

"No, I haven't had any dreams about her, nothing, nothing at all." I was really quite disappointed as, being Lisa's mother, I would have thought I would be the one to have had vivid dreams, but nothing at all had occurred.

It was a few weeks later, during the early hours, that I was suddenly woken up by Roger sitting up in bed, crying. "I've just had a vivid dream that I was driving along this street and I saw Lisa. I stopped to give her a lift and she got in and sat behind me. Then she put her arms around me and asked me if I was all right. I attempted a reply, but the reply was drowned by my tears - and I woke up suddenly - sobbing, with tears running down my face." The dream was so vivid and real.

Frances had not only had a vivid dream of Lisa, but also strange happenings were taking place in her house. This is her account of what happened on several occasions:

"Michael was away on business. I got up at 7.00 am and went downstairs to find that the video recorder was on and recording. The 'timer record' button was on so I phoned Michael to find out what he was recording. He didn't know what I was talking about. I had gone to bed the previous evening making sure everything was switched off, including the video. I didn't know how to set the timer on the video and I certainly know that the children didn't do it. It was recording the news.

"On another occasion I'd taken the children to school and playschool, and bought a few things from the shop and returned home. When it was time to fetch Peter from playschool, I realised I couldn't find my purse. I looked in the usual places that I could have left it but it wasn't there. I phoned the shops I'd been in but no one had seen it. For some reason I decided to look in the unit in the sitting room. I didn't for one second think that it would be in there but when I opened the drawer, there it was. I had never put my purse in there before and I never have since!

"During one morning, the house began to feel very cold. I turned the heating control up but it didn't make any difference. I rang Michael to tell him, thinking the central heating had broken down. He told me to check the central heating switch in the kitchen. I had forgotten about this as nobody had ever touched it. It was out of the way under the wall cupboards. It was switched off when I checked. I know I didn't switch it off and as the children were not at home I know they hadn't touched it!

"It was Boxing Day and we were going over to Mum and Roger's for lunch. I had arranged to give Mum three rings on the phone when we left (the journey would take approximately forty-five minutes). About five minutes after we had left, I realised I had forgotten to ring Mum. Michael asked if I wanted to go back home or stop off at a call box (this was before mobile phones!) I said no and that I was sure it would be okay. Anyway, when we arrived I told Mum how sorry I was that I hadn't called. She looked surprised and said that I did call and that she had been expecting us to arrive at that time. Apparently Mum had received three rings, and when she answered nobody was there and she thought it was me giving her the signal that we had just left home!"

I remember this latter incident and how surprised I was to hear that Frances had forgotten to phone, but I also remember thinking, what a coincidence! I wonder if it was, just as the incidents at Frances's home remain a mystery, or whether it was Lisa playing tricks again.

At around the same time that Lisa died, a toddler was murdered in terrible circumstances and I remember thinking that we must count our blessings to enable us to get through the days. Lisa had not been murdered or mutilated or her body violated in any way and we should be thankful for that small mercy. It is impossible to imagine how the families of such victims can live with those memories. My heart goes out to parents who have to cope with such terrible tragedies, as I don't know how they manage.

I felt I had to do something to take my mind off my grief, and I decided to apply for voluntary work in our local hospice. There I helped the nurses tend to the sick and also took part in fund-raising. It was a wonderful experience and I met such lovely, brave people, and far from being a sad place it was filled with laughter and hope. Sometimes I would sit by a patient and chat about all sorts of things, and one time I found myself saying to a lovely man who hadn't got long to live that one day he would see all his loved ones again!

"Do you really think so?" he asked, his eyes so full of expectation.

"Yes, I am sure you will," I replied, wanting to give him the reassurance that he badly needed.

"If only I could really believe that," he said wistfully.

Our pain and anguish were still very much with us, as it was still early days. I was enjoying my work in the hospice and I was able to concentrate on trying to give comfort to others, which did help as it stopped me from thinking of myself all the time. I suppose it was a sort of healing for me. I still relished the solitude on my walks with the dogs, but now I also sang one of the hymns that we had sung in church and I still sing it to this day when I am feeling a bit low:

> *Shall we gather at the river*
> *Where bright angel feet have trod*
> *With its crystal tide forever*
> *Flowing by the throne of God?*

> *Yes we'll gather at the river*
> *The beautiful, the beautiful river*
> *Gather with the saints at the river*
> *That flows by the throne of God.*

As a good friend of ours said, "It is a good happy clappy hymn!" However, it does the trick for me, and it is also one of those tunes that keeps repeating itself in my head. The words are lovely and there are several more verses which I have refrained from adding!

Shortly after Lisa died, we learnt of many more deaths that had resulted from carbon monoxide poisoning, mainly students who were living in rented accommodation in the cities, and we were told that some parents had set up a carbon monoxide awareness group. We were appalled at the number that had died, as there was no legislation in place at that time to make landlords responsible for maintaining gas appliances correctly. One couple had two sons - one was studying at university and the other had gone to visit him, and they both died. The tragedy for this family was too awful to imagine, leaving both parents completely broken by their sons' deaths. As a group we tried so hard to raise awareness of the danger of carbon monoxide, but our battle with the authorities was far from an easy one. It was costing a lot of money to keep up the pressure on companies to produce the necessary alarms - they had to pass rigorous British Safety Standards and that would take years. However, a few months after Lisa's death legislation was passed that made it law for every landlord to have a certificate to show that all heating appliances had been properly serviced. To this day, it is very doubtful if this legislation is being properly enforced by unscrupulous landlords. The number of rented rooms in every city being used by students is enormous and deaths are still occurring, but not in such large numbers as before. Today, there are carbon monoxide alarms on the market, so if you know of any student living in a rented property, please make sure that they have one fitted. Death by this deadly gas is silent - you just fall asleep.

We began to look forward to our visits to the Spiritualist church, just in case Lisa should happen to come through with a message for us. Yes, we were vulnerable and grieving, but not stupid, and we did not accept everything that was told to us by some of the mediums we met. However, the concept of Spiritualism was arousing our curiosity and we decided that if we were going to continue to go to Una's church then we would also read as much as we could of its history and how it had evolved. I had read all of Doris Stokes' books and hers was one of the last books that Lisa had read before she died - she had asked me if she could borrow it from me the last time she was home. I must admit that her request surprised me, as it was not the sort of book I thought she would be interested in - her reading matter was usually dancing-related books!

Una took the service as usual on Sunday and Steve was the demonstrating medium. We loved his prayers as they were so spontaneous and straight from the heart. I'm afraid the repetitious prayers we had been used to all our lives didn't have such an impact on us and quite honestly I found some very difficult to understand. My tears still came uninvited during the hymns; the words were so poignant and the effect they had on me was to last for some time. Listening to Steve, we noticed that it was only very occasionally that there was a 'no' (i.e. when the message means nothing to anyone in the audience) unlike other visiting mediums when the 'nos' were far more frequent. He often shared some philosophy before starting his mediumship, which we found very interesting and comforting, a lot better than some of the long sermons that didn't quite 'hit the mark' with us.

Again we chatted with Steve after the service and it wasn't long before we invited him to come home with us for some refreshment. Little did we realise that that first evening would be the start of many that led to our having long discussions late into the night over more than the odd glass of home-made wine! We were learning more and more about the gift that some people have, and I say 'some' reservedly, as there are I am sure many more who have experienced phenomena and don't wish to talk about it. Roger and I were fascinated by Steve, who actually heard voices from those who had passed on. This was amazing - perhaps he would hear something from Lisa! But we also learnt that Steve could not demand someone to speak to him; he just had to wait and see who came through before he passed on their message. We often wondered whether Lisa was trying to get through to us and whether the lifelike vivid dreams that were experienced by Roger and Frances were an indication that Lisa was trying to communicate with them.

A few months after Lisa's death, we received a letter from The Central School of Ballet, inviting us down to a special performance to be given by members of Lisa's ballet class and asking whether I would present the cups that were being awarded to some of her fellow pupils. We accepted with pleasure, but when I arrived at the school my emotions took over and I'm afraid I spent most of the afternoon crying. The young children, most of them around seven or eight years old, performed a special dance that had been choreographed for them in memory of Lisa. They danced beautifully; Lisa would have been so proud of them. The time came for me to present the awards, and when the first little one came up to me both of us had tears streaming down our cheeks. Then they all came over to me, most of them crying; they had loved Lisa so much and missed her terribly. I turned to go back to my seat, thinking what an awful mess I had made of presenting the prizes, but I hoped that everybody would understand, and I also hoped that Lisa was around to see how much she had been loved by all the children.

A few weeks later we travelled to Bedford College for an afternoon performance given by the pupils of the college in memory of Lisa. It was a lovely gesture, as Lisa had been very popular, and it was extra special as Roger's family, who lived not too far away, were also there to share with us a special occasion, and this time I didn't disgrace myself!

CHAPTER 6

One Sunday evening at home Steve suggested that Roger and I should experience other Spiritualist churches and that he could come with us when he was demonstrating there. It was apparent that Steve was popular with a lot of the churches around the Yorkshire area and during the next couple of years we visited many different places, sometimes to hear other mediums, but mostly to watch Steve demonstrating. We loved the way he put his hand to his ear as if to hear more clearly what was being said, and the way he walked up and down at great speed, leaving everyone amazed at his energy! Other mediums would sometimes talk about auras and how one was going to live a long life, but this did nothing for us. We wanted proof that there was an afterlife, not a health check! We have since learnt that mediumship is communication with a disincarnate body, whereas a psychic picks up things from your aura to give you a reading but is not actually in touch with those who have passed on. I'm afraid that many psychics think that they are mediums as well, but this is not always the case.

We had been reading as much as we could. We found Arthur Findlay's *On the Edge of the Etheric* especially interesting at that time as we were so new to the idea of Spiritualism, and one of his other books, *The Rock of Truth*, describing the history of religion, helped us in our quest to understand how different religions came about over many centuries. What we read made sense to us and we found this to be quite a relief as, although both of us had been educated to believe in life after death, it was always on the basis of faith as there was no proof. The Bible is the word of God, and not to be questioned: this is the concept preached by many orthodox religions. But we believe that many people do require proof and that not only is it natural to question but also it is the right of every individual to do so. We questioned what Steve was doing many times and would often stop and ask each other, "What are we becoming involved with?" Each time we came back to the same question: what is it that Steve is hearing and how can he be getting it so right each time? And the only answer was: there must be someone telling him these things! Steve had become a good friend to us over that last terrible year and had helped us so much with our grief. He had shared with us his knowledge that our earthly life is not the end and that no one can die.

One day Steve asked me if I would do a bit on philosophy in the churches before his demonstrations. He explained that it would give him time to have a cigarette to calm his nerves and also a few moments of quiet time beforehand. The joy he brought to those lucky enough to receive a message was obvious, and when I started my philosophy I tried to emphasise the importance of being a good medium as paramount. People like me wanted the truth, not an embellishment of a medium's own ideas of what they thought we wanted to hear - we wanted to know for certain that our loved ones were still there for us and, above all, to receive personal proof. That way, mediums give us hope and knowledge that life is worth living after all and that there is purpose to our being here on this earth. It was after one service that a lady came up to me and said that she had been on the point of giving up her mediumship, but having listened to me she felt she had been given renewed strength to continue to help those that had been bereaved. Well, I thought, at least someone understood what I was trying to say!

Although it was agreed with Steve that I should speak for just a short time, to me it seemed like an age! As I had acted on the stage in amateur dramatics for several years, facing an audience didn't worry me. What concerned me most was what I was actually going to say. Besides stressing the importance of being a good medium, the rest seemed to come from somewhere, as I never rehearsed anything. Perhaps I had my own guide watching over me! Steve, to settle his nerves before a demonstration, often used those minutes to ask for help from his guides. However, he didn't have the confidence that they would always be there for him, as he never took them for granted.

We were growing accustomed to our new way of thinking and found it very comforting to know that Lisa was still around us, although we still hadn't received any message from her. We wanted to find out more about the different types of Spiritualism and one Sunday I had the opportunity to go and see Ursula Roberts giving a demonstration of trance at a church in Leeds. We were a bit apprehensive as we didn't know quite what to expect. We had been told that we should remain very quiet, as the medium could suffer from shock if abruptly awakened from the trance. As we took our seats, we were all told that we would have the opportunity to ask questions if we so wished at the end of the demonstration. An elderly lady approached the podium and sat facing us; it wasn't long before she started to speak in a low, masculine voice. I was fascinated by her voice and wished that I had heard her speak normally before she'd gone into trance, just for comparison. I cannot remember what was said, but I do know that I did not understand much at that point, and it seemed to go on for a very long time. When it came to question time, I put my hand up.

"Do we die alone?" I asked, knowing that Lisa had been by herself in the bathroom and it had been upsetting for me to think of her with nobody with her.

The answer was, "There is always someone to guide you over, so you are not alone."

I wondered who would have met her and guided her over as all her close family were still alive. Before I could ask anything more, Ursula (or whoever had taken her over) spoke again.

"I believe you have had some communication already?"

"No I haven't," I replied.

"Then it must have been too early for you," came the response.

And that was that. After answering several more questions from the audience, Ursula came out of her trance and the evening ended.

Looking back on that evening, yes it was interesting to experience, but I still wanted something more definite. Roger said he found it all a bit beyond him and I think he was also disappointed that the evening hadn't been more exciting as neither of us really understood what had happened.

We continued going to the Spiritualist church every Sunday and on one occasion we met a young medium, Cathy, and her boyfriend, who talked about healing and how they held a healing sanctuary at her home every month. Many people attended, and some took along their pets if they needed healing. We were very interested in what they had to say and invited them back to the cottage for our usual Sunday evening discussions. They arrived the following Sunday and made themselves comfortable on the sofa, while Steve decided to sit cross-legged on the floor opposite them and I sat at one end of the room and Roger at the other. We were all chatting to one another when suddenly, without warning, Cathy went into a trance and started speaking with a Chinese accent. I wasn't quite sure what to say or do, but we were assured by her boyfriend that this happened frequently. "Thank you for coming sir," he addressed his girlfriend. I felt uneasy, even embarrassed as Steve caught my eye and gave a slight shake of his head. The conversation between the Chinese person and her boyfriend continued, with a lot of 'no sir' and 'yes sir' and then, just as suddenly as she had gone into trance, she came out of it. "Coffee?" I asked and disappeared into the kitchen relieved to be somewhere else. Roger joined me and asked me what on earth that was all about, and we both had a feeling that something just wasn't quite right. The trance sessions happened several times throughout the evening and it was after the couple had left that we asked Steve what he thought about it all. "Didn't believe any of it," he said. Well, we thought, who are we to argue? He should know! But I knew that I was interested in the healing at Cathy's home and decided that we would at least pay a visit and perhaps take along our Labrador who was suffering from arthritis in his hips.

It was a month or so later that Roger and I made the trip

to Cathy's home, taking Paddy with us. It had been arranged that we should arrive at a certain time, as the healer, who had a sanctuary in London, was extremely popular and people from a wide area came to see him.

We drove around the estate looking for Cathy's house which, after asking several people for directions, we eventually found tucked away at the end of a tiny cul-de-sac. We knocked on what we thought was the front door several times to no avail when a voice, with a German accent, shouted, "Go away!" Roger backed away quickly as the voice sounded quite angry. "Let's go round the back," I suggested. Luckily we found some other people approaching and followed them through the back door. There were about a dozen chairs placed around the kitchen and into the hallway, most of them taken. We were the only ones with a pet, so we manoeuvred ourselves into a corner with Paddy wondering what was going to happen next!

Several people came and went to and from a side room and it became obvious that this was where the healer was working. We were told by a lady sitting next to us that this was quite a regular occurrence for her and she always came when the doctor was there. "Doctor?" I queried. "Yes, the healer is taken over by a German doctor whose name is Dr Khan. He is wonderful. Dr Khan has helped me so much with my cancer." So that explained the guttural voice that had shouted at us to 'go away' - we had obviously been knocking on the door to his room where he was busy working.

We waited about half an hour before the 'doctor' came out to look at Paddy. In a strong German accent he asked us about Paddy's condition and he placed his hands on Paddy's head. "He is a good dog." "Yes, he is a lovely dog," I said. I felt strange knowing that here was an Englishman who had actually been taken over by this German Doctor Khan, and I really didn't know what else to say! He gently put his hands all over Paddy's body, and Paddy never moved; he seemed to know that here was a very special man who was trying to help him with the pain in his hips.

On the way home, Paddy slept peacefully in the back of the car. We were desperately hoping that something, whatever it was, might have happened to help our lovely old dog with his pain. I silently said a little prayer: "Please, whoever you are, wherever you are, help Paddy get better, and Lisa, if you are around, please help him as well."

CHAPTER 7

Steve became a very good friend to us in the months following Lisa's death. He was introducing us gradually to a new way of thinking about our life, the purpose we have on earth and how our loved ones remain around us. We found it difficult at times to accept all these new ideas that we were hearing and experiencing, but we remained open minded. Those evenings that we had when Steve spoke to us of his guides and how they worked with him, and how he had experienced out-of-the-ordinary happenings in his own life, will always remain with us as wonderful memories. But, more to the point, they were also playing a part in our healing, as the pain was still very much with us, never diminishing; there were still the bad days when tears would come with no prompting.

Steve also introduced us to some of his medium friends and we listened and learnt how Spirit works in many different ways. One of his friends, Maureen, had been a medium and healer for many years and she asked Roger if he had ever tried healing. This was something that neither of us had had any experience of, and so Roger was of course rather reticent with his answer, but Maureen was adamant that he should try. It was very strange that she should have mentioned about healing, because we had been to a couple of demonstrations during the week and both mediums had approached Roger to ask if he was a healer. Again Roger had said "No", so when Maureen talked about healing we began to take a bit more notice! You will observe that we were still very cautious at this stage and didn't jump up and down with excitement. This idea was still very new to us and we were just finding out so much that sometimes it was all too overwhelming to take in. Also, we had not discussed our thoughts or findings with any of the family except for Lesley and Frances, as there was still this awkwardness within us in regard to talking about Spiritualism.

I have spoken about the vivid dreams that Frances and Roger experienced and as yet I hadn't encountered anything that I could definitely say was Lisa trying to communicate. It is extraordinary how some friends, after Lisa's death, suddenly found the courage to confide in us that they had actually seen the spirit of a family member. We realised that they were trying to comfort us by sharing the knowledge that there is no death and that Lisa was still actually around us. However, we were amazed at how many of them had seen either the spirit of their beloved dog who had died years ago or their grandmother or grandfather.

One very great friend of ours, who was a lay preacher at our Methodist church, confided to us that she had actually seen her son who had died at a very young age. She knew it was her son as he was the spitting image of her husband! There is absolutely no reason to believe that she did not see her son - to her it was so natural - and the same applies to Lisa's very great school friend. She told us that she was working abroad as a dancer when sadly her beloved dog died at home. On returning from abroad, she paid a visit to her grandma and was helping with the washing up. For some reason she turned around from the sink, to see her dog lying on the floor with his head on his paws looking up at her, before fading away. Again, there is no reason for Lisa's friend to have made this up, as there was nothing to gain by doing so. I will also mention that my sister swears that she saw our grandmother at the foot of her bed shortly after she had died, and we believe her - why not?

I could mention many others who have told us about seeing spirits, but the point I am trying to get across is that all these people have no reason to lie. They all felt completely at ease with their experience. As for myself, I'm sorry, I don't have anything to report - I wish I did!

After Maureen told Roger that he should try healing, we thought it would be a good idea for Paddy to have healing for his hip problem. He had been on tablets for quite some time to ease the pain, but the vet had recently told us that Paddy's liver was reacting adversely to them and that he should come off them for the time being. Both dogs slept in our bedroom at night, one at each side of the bed on their own cushions. Paddy slept on Roger's side and Rupert on mine. This was the best arrangement as Roger was a sound sleeper, so Paddy's restlessness hardly ever woke him up.

On one particular night, when both dogs were settled, Roger decided to try his healing on Paddy. In his own words, "I placed my right hand (right, because it felt most natural for me) about two inches above Paddy's hips and, in my mind, asked for any healing help that could be given to me. Initially, Paddy looked round at me as if to say, "What on earth are you doing?", but then he put his head back down quite happily. I don't know what I expected, and I felt almost silly at first, until I started to feel slight 'pin-pricks' in my palm. I guessed that my hand must be touching Paddy's hair but, no, it was still a couple of inches above his hips. I kept this up for about five minutes, and decided that I would start to do this at any time of the day or night for Paddy, to help him in any way I could. That was the start of a regular 'session' for Pad. As time went on, we noticed that Pad seemed to be more comfortable - he wasn't on tablets, and neither was he yelping in pain!! This was Roger's first venture into healing and it became obvious that it must have been helping Paddy because for the next eighteen months he was free of both tablets and pain!

We were making a lot of new friends at the church, and on one Sunday a lady brought along her niece who apparently, we were told, could see Spirit and had been able to do so from a very young age. Karina was a shy, pretty twelve-year-old, and she was completely unaware that she had a very special gift as it was all so natural to her. It was fascinating to hear how she had had the company of a spirit lady right from when she was little. She didn't know who it was and had no knowledge of why she was around her but had accepted her as a friend. During the service we found it quite amazing that Karina could actually see those that wanted to pass on messages through the medium, lining up awaiting their turn! When Steve was demonstrating she said that there was somebody who followed him closely and we thought it could be one of his many guides, although it could also have been one of those who was desperate to pass on their message. Interestingly, Steve was totally unaware of anybody following him.

When Steve was demonstrating, his energy left us in awe. He paced back and forth, pausing only to grab a quick drink of water or listen to any responses from the congregation. He frequently put his hand to his ear as if to hear more clearly - as he explained, it was like listening to a muffled voice at times and it could sometimes be difficult to decipher. Later, after the service, I asked Karina's aunt if she would be interested in coming back to our house sometime as I longed to know if Karina would be able to see Lisa around us. She said that she would have to ask her mother who, we were told, did not believe in anything to do with Spiritualism, and therefore Karina had to keep quiet about her spirit companion and confide only in her aunt. We felt quite excited about her coming round and were so relieved when permission was given, and a Sunday was quickly arranged.

During the service on the Sunday that Karina was coming to the cottage, I sat next to her and asked her what she was seeing. "People are queuing up by the door. Someone is in charge of them," she said. I wanted to ask more - my curiosity was getting the better of me - but the service was about to start and I controlled myself unwillingly. It was difficult to believe that this young girl could actually see spirit people while I could neither sense nor see anything. I wondered how many other people in the church could also see the spirit people lining up to speak with their loved ones.

Why did we believe her? What made us so eager to believe her? I can hear some sceptical readers saying that it was because we were feeling vulnerable and were clinging on to the idea that our Lisa was still around us. However, my answer to that is, yes, we were very much in the early stages of our new thinking about life after our earthly death and were hoping that it was true that Lisa was still around. But - and it is a very big but - we were also very discerning and did not take everything we heard to heart. We were still analysing what we were being told, as we had to find a

Left: Lisa training her pupils during her Summer holiday 'Good toes and naughty toes'

Right: Lisa in November 1978, aged 11

Below: Posing for Roger during her practice sessions

Above: Lisa on holiday at Court Gardens Farm, aged 18

Right: Lesley and Lisa with Frances on her wedding day

Below: A scene from 'Helen Keller', a ballet which she choreographed and won a special award

Above: Lisa and her diploma, 1989

Left: Steve, Jill and Roger before an evening at Plinston Hall

logical answer to this business of still living on after discarding our earthly bodies. This was a new venture for the two of us and we were both going to give it a fair hearing!

We arrived home later that evening with Karina and her aunt. I sat Karina next to me and Roger sat next to her aunt on the sofa. I began to ask Karina if she could see anything in the room when she interrupted me.

"There's somebody standing by the door."

I shivered, not out of fear but out of excitement, and glanced at Roger, who was looking very apprehensive.

"I think it's Lisa. She is listening to us," Karina continued.

"Well, she can listen as much as she likes, and she is welcome," I said - if only I could see her! - "How do you know it is Lisa as you have never met her?" I asked. There were so many other questions I wanted to ask, but I didn't know where to begin.

"She lived here," Karina replied. "Why is Lisa holding two babies in her arms?" she continued. "She is saying, 'It's all your fault, Mum'."

I was startled to hear this. I had had two miscarriages many years previously, but there's no way that Karina would have known about it.

I explained to Karina why there were two babies and then I asked, "What is Lisa wearing?"

"A blue dress," was the reply.

"Where is she living?"

"She lives in a flat with others."

I thought this very strange as I was sure Lisa would have liked a little cottage somewhere in the country; however, I realised that that would have been my idea of a perfect home.

"Is she still there?"

"Yes."

"Do you believe that we lead many lives, Karina."

"Yes," she replied. "Shall I tell you about yours?"

This was getting interesting. Karina said that she would ask her companion to get the information for us, as apparently it is all written down in a book and would have to be looked up. It transpired that her companion was always with her to protect her, and it seemed that there was an unspoken conversation between the two of them, as Karina said that she had gone to look in the book! Her aunt took all of this in her stride; she was so used to Karina's gift as she herself had been helped with problems in her life and had got accustomed to this lady that was always around Karina, although she had never seen her for herself. Eventually, Karina's companion returned and I was told that in a previous life I had been shot as a very young child. In one of Roger's past lives he had been involved in a boating accident. We found this all very interesting, as we had said nothing to either Karina or her aunt about our personal lives or situation. However, I did wonder if my past life could account for my very real fear of guns!

The following week when attending church Karina asked us quite innocently, "Why did Lisa call you Mum but called Roger by his name instead of Dad?"

CHAPTER 8

Whatever our thoughts about that evening with Karina and her aunt, her innocent remark left a tremendous impression on us. There was no way that Karina knew anything about my divorce from the children's biological father and that Roger had taken on all four of us many years ago! As far as Karina was concerned, Roger was Lisa's father, so had Lisa really been standing by the door watching and listening to us? We like to think so.

It was during the week that Roger had to go into the office in Huddersfield when he felt a sudden urge to give Steve a ring. He wasn't due to give him a call, but the feeling was overwhelming. He didn't know why, because the middle of office hours was an unusual time to phone, but he rang Steve. He made some excuse for the call and as they were chatting Steve mentioned that they had just had the decorators in to paint the sitting room and he said he was feeling fed up because the wall above their fire was already black. Roger immediately had an uneasy feeling and asked Steve if he had noticed anything else unusual.

"Yes, Caroline is having bad headaches and hasn't been feeling too well."

"Steve, you must phone the Gas Board and get them to come and check your fire, and tell them about the black mark on the wall."

The gasman came out very quickly and, checking behind the fire, found rubble blocking the chimney. The gas was cut off immediately due to the leakage of carbon monoxide fumes, which had also been the cause of Caroline's headaches. Why did Roger have an overwhelming desire to phone Steve? Had Lisa somehow been trying to get through to him? We can guess, but we will never know for certain.

When Steve was demonstrating he said that he could often sense Lisa standing behind him but that she wouldn't come forward. This was in keeping with her character, as I have mentioned before, because she would never push herself forward, so it did seem reasonable that she should still have the same characteristics. Also Roger and I, by this time, had come to accept that our lives are not just snuffed out, but that we do carry on, although on a different vibration. Steve's clairaudience was proof to us that Spirit was communicating with him and the spirits he was listening to did indeed live at one time on this earth. Also, if there isn't anything at the end, why bother to go through all the ups and miserable downs in life? The gift of clairaudience that Steve has gives so much proof of survival after death for the lucky people that receive a message. It is the small personal things that are relayed, which nobody else could possibly have knowledge of, that provide the proof. We learnt that the spiritual life ahead of us is determined by the life we live here and now. We have personal responsibility for our own life, so we cannot put the blame on anyone else for our actions! We were also learning so much from Arthur Findlay's books. He was a sceptic until one day he met a medium who told him facts about his dead father that only he knew. This aroused his curiosity and so he attended a Spiritualist church to learn more and then spent the rest of his life on a quest to find the truth about life after death.

We were still visiting other churches and I was doing my bit on philosophy before Steve did his demonstrations. His reputation was growing and he started to work outside the church, sharing the evening with other mediums, and he was also doing much for charity together with Una.

At one of the venues, Huddersfield College, Steve had agreed to work with another medium, Paul Norton, and he asked that Paul should start the evening. They both sat on the stage, and we waited in anticipation for Steve's turn. Paul was quite good and kept the small audience's attention, while Steve sat and waited, and we waited and waited for Steve to get up. But Steve didn't get up at all that evening and when we asked why afterwards he simply said that he didn't get anything to say. That is the first and only time we have ever witnessed Steve being at a loss for words! However, that is one of the reasons we admire him - he is honest and has integrity. Someone else could easily have taken the stage regardless and waffled their way through.

It was at Rotherham Arts Centre where we met another well-known medium, Val Williams. She was working with Steve and she was also known for having one-to-one sessions. This intrigued me as Roger and I had never been to a 'one to one'. I decided to pay Val a visit when she was at home, hoping, like many others before me, that I would be told something that would provide proof of an afterlife. Val was very welcoming and immediately put me at my ease. After half an hour of mentioning so many names that I couldn't relate to, I left feeling very despondent. This visit was one of many 'one to ones' that Roger and I had with various mediums over the years, some of whom came recommended by people that had been and were suitably impressed with the outcome. However, we can honestly say that we personally haven't had any satisfactory meetings with anyone and we have always come away with the feeling: why on earth did we bother?!

Steve was leaving us to discover more about the different aspects of Spiritualism and didn't discourage us from seeing these other mediums; indeed, he was always very interested in what we had to say about our experiences! In fact he was very encouraging if we suggested going to see a particular medium and occasionally he would come along if his time allowed. Steve was working full time as a hairdresser in Leeds and his evenings and weekends were taken up with his spiritual work and so he had very little time to himself. However, when Stephen O'Brien held a demonstration in Leeds, our Steve decided to come along with us on that evening.

We chose to sit separately that evening to see if a link could be made between us, so Steve sat on the opposite side of the theatre to where we were sitting. Roger and I had decided to sit together and we were listening to some messages being given out when Stephen O'Brien said something that made me put my hand up quickly. I cannot remember now what the message was about, but Stephen stopped in the middle of what he was saying and said that he felt an energy coming from the other side of the theatre. He said that there was a sort of triangle and it was confusing him. This was the first time this had happened to him and he couldn't make sense of it, but it was a definite triangle of energy. Roger and I sat there and didn't enlighten him to the fact that our Stephen was sitting just the other side of the aisle, as we wanted to be told more, but unfortunately no more was forthcoming!

I was disappointed that nothing more was said, as again we had been looking for a tangible sign that Lisa might have come through to us. Also the fact that the theatre was so large and it was full to capacity meant that the responses from people went unheard for a lot of the audience and we felt lost amongst the large crowd that attended. The smaller and more intimate demonstrations that our Steve gave made all the difference to the atmosphere of the evening and we felt as if we could share in the joy of other's messages and their responses.

Comparing Steve's demonstrations and the staged version with Stephen O'Brien, they was as different as chalk and cheese. Both mediums have a wonderful gift, but one is 'what you see is what you get, warts and all' and the other is stage managed to produce a very slick presentation - I know which we prefer!

CHAPTER 9

Roger had been giving Paddy his healing regularly and, much to our delight, Paddy was able to continue with his daily walks and run around with Rupert without pain. He was stiff afterwards, but he was enjoying life without taking any of the tablets to ease his arthritis.

One night, as the dogs lay on their beds, Paddy was obviously feeling rather restless and, as he was shifting around on his bed, he woke Roger, who looked to see what he was doing. Much to Roger's amazement he saw blue lights around each paw. Could it have been static electricity? I wondered when Roger told me in the morning. Roger said that they were definitely blue lights that lingered for some moments as Paddy settled himself. We had been told that blue is the colour of healing - and we have often wondered whether the lights were due to the healing that Roger had been giving Paddy.

We had another fifteen months with Paddy before one Saturday morning he decided that he could no longer be bothered to get up from his bed to eat or go for his walk, both of which he loved. We had often said that we would know when his time had come, because he wouldn't want to do either. He had been losing weight over the previous few weeks and sadly it was now obvious to both of us that Paddy had called it a day. He had been with us for fifteen years, since he was eight weeks old, and had been both a wonderful companion and a handsome and proud golden Labrador.

Our vet, who had attended to Paddy for several years, had already told us that when the time came he would like to be the one to come out to put him to sleep. But it was also the day that Steve was getting married to Caroline. They had been together for some time and we had been invited to the wedding, but this was also going to be the day we had to say goodbye to our Paddy.

The vet arrived. We knelt down by Paddy's head, talking to him and stroking him and saying what a wonderful dog he had been. I asked Lisa, "If you are around, please take Paddy to be with you", and if she was there I am sure that is what she would have done, because she loved him as much as we did. He died within seconds of being given the injection.

We had put Rupert in the car to avoid any disturbance and upset for either of them, and now we let him into the house after the vet had taken Paddy away. His natural instinct was to search for his friend and he went to every room looking for Paddy. They had been inseparable - Paddy was the top dog and Rupert was lost without him.

Once again we were grieving and as we drove to Steve and Caroline's wedding with Rupert in the back of the car, tears poured down our faces, but we knew we had done the right thing. It was supposed to be a happy journey to Steve's wedding, but for both of us the tears would not stop flowing. When we arrived Steve was waiting in the church looking very handsome in his tails, and the place was full of family and friends. Caroline arrived looking radiant and seemed to have so many bridesmaids following her up the aisle. It was a lovely wedding, and throughout the reception Roger and I took it in turns to return to the car to make sure that

Rupert was all right and to have another weep in private. The familiar pain of grief was back and it would stay with us for a long time. Rupert became very dependent on me, and I replaced Paddy as top dog. He never left my side from that day.

Every weekend we visited Lisa's garden and wondered whether she now had our two cats and Paddy as well as the two lost babies to look after - she was going to be kept busy! Steve's conviction that Lisa was still around and hadn't left us gave us renewed strength every day. I still sang the hymns on my walks and talked to Lisa at home, and so did Roger, but we were now beginning to be able to laugh at some of the jokes she had told. She had a wicked sense of humour, but we still hadn't had a personal message from her through Steve or any other medium. Neither had we talked to members of our family about our questioning and visiting Spiritualist churches. We didn't feel comfortable with the idea of discussing what we were doing, because we felt at the time that both sets of parents would not be quite as 'open minded' as us on that particular subject.

We thought back to the time, not many months earlier, when Steve told us that we would be working with Spirit one day and my response had been very negative. Now we were becoming more involved by finding out more for ourselves and helping Steve reach out to people who had been bereaved, and were questioning like us. I remember talking to a patient in the hospice who had throat cancer and hadn't long to live. I was sitting by his bed chatting and he said that he was afraid of dying as he didn't know what lay ahead for him.

"Do you believe in an afterlife?" I asked, thinking that

perhaps I could mention what Roger and I had found out from Steve.

"I'm not sure. I think there is something, but I don't know," he replied.

I told him about Lisa and how we had found a new friend who had shown us through his gift of clairaudience that there is certainly an afterlife. I explained that Steve could not initiate contact with those that had passed on but that they contacted him and he relayed their messages. As I was telling him this, I felt surprised that I was actually talking about spirits to a stranger!

But this lovely man listened and then said, "Do you really believe that?"

"Yes," I replied, and I really did believe it now.

I do hope that he found some peace with the thought that one day he too could come back to talk with his loved ones.

* * *

It was in December that Roger's parents came to stay for the weekend. It was my birthday and they had come to celebrate it with us. By that time it was almost two years since Lisa had passed on.

It had been snowing the previous night and I volunteered to take Rupert for his daily walk before going out for my birthday lunch. Rupert and I followed our usual tracks through the wood until we reached the familiar fork in the path where I paused, wondering if I should take the shorter way back home or the longer one which meant crossing a large field. I decided to take the route across the field, as this would give Rupert plenty of exercise. Being a lurcher he was always full of energy and appreciated any extra exercise we could give him. Having climbed over the stile into the field, I began the trek uphill. As I reached the middle of the field, and looking down at the snow, something rather curious made me stop. Just ahead of me I noticed large letters etched into the snow, but there were no footprints around either leading towards or away from them. I walked forwards to have a closer look and, much to my amazement, they spelled out a girl's name ... 'LISA'. I didn't think it was too extraordinary at the time, as to me it was obvious that somebody had stamped out their name. I told Roger on my return home, who was rather amazed at the coincidences that had occurred: after all, IT WAS MY BIRTHDAY and also I needn't have taken that particular route home - AND, of all the girls' names to choose from, the name was LISA! I think what surprised me more at the time was that I couldn't see any footprints anywhere in the snow, which I would have expected. Steve was equally amazed at the 'coincidences', as he doesn't believe in them and has always maintained that everything happens for a reason! Maybe Lisa was wishing me a happy birthday after all! I like to think so.

It was over that weekend that we mentioned to Roger's parents about our friend Steve and told them about his gift and what happens at a Spiritualist church. We were hoping to be able to talk about the things we had experienced and to discuss and exchange ideas about it all. But the matter was quickly dismissed and it was made clear to both of us that this was of no interest to them. In fact, the whole idea of Spiritualism was just too strange. We have never mentioned it again in their company.

It was a few weeks later, when Roger was reading the

magazine *Psychic World*, that he noticed the name of Judith Chisholm. On an impulse he decided to contact her and tell her about Steve and his work, and also how impressed we had been and how we were now helping him. Judith replied immediately and enquired whether, if she could find a venue in London, Steve would be prepared to go down and give a demonstration. We put the idea to Steve, explaining that Judith had kindly offered to put us all up for the night, including Rupert. His reaction was enthusiastic, and so we waited until Judith had tracked down a suitable venue. She found an old theatre in Islington not far from where she lived, which she felt would be ideal. Settling on a date, we began to tell our friends around that area of Steve's imminent arrival. Some of the people that we mentioned it to were members of the carbon monoxide awareness group and a few replied that they would be very interested in coming along. One of the replies that we had was from the couple who had lost both their sons. How wonderful it would be, we thought, if they were to receive a message via Steve. We never told Steve that they were expected to be at the evening; in fact we never told him anything about their circumstances, as any message he gave out would then be proof to us as well as to them.

Arriving at Hoxton Hall that evening, a couple of hours before Steve was demonstrating, we were met by litter a foot deep outside the theatre. We were aghast until we learnt that the market had been there that day and we were assured that it was going to be cleared shortly. We breathed a sigh of relief, having started wondering what we had all let ourselves in for!

Roger and Judith were doing all the organising and I left

them together with Steve and went to seek out a secluded spot where I could stay with Rupert. We found a place behind the stage and I put his bed down, and he was quite happy to curl up and go to sleep so long as I stayed with him. The theatre began to fill up and I had no idea who had arrived. I just hoped that the couple who had lost their sons had managed to come along. Roger joined me at the back and Judith went on stage to introduce Steve.

Everything was going very smoothly, the messages were being accepted and Steve was in fine form. He was in the middle of a message when suddenly we heard him say, "You have lost a son. I feel as if I'm choking." The message continued, with Steve mentioning many points to which the couple could relate. Then all of a sudden Steve said to them, "There is another one here. Have you lost two sons?"

Roger and I couldn't believe it. Steve was giving a message to the couple who had lost both their sons. He went on to give a lovely message about their daughter and a wedding and said that their sons had been there. We never saw them afterwards, but I do hope that in their grief they were able to see that Steve had brought them a genuine message from their sons, and hopefully it provided them with a small grain of comfort.

It was a very successful evening and we thanked Judith for her hospitality, as she had lost one of her sons not long before that and so it was obviously a very difficult time for her. She was also developing an interest in EVP (Electronic Voice Phenomena) and has since written a book about it entitled *Voices from Paradise*. It is certainly an interesting read, and demonstrates another source of communication with Spirit, and Judith has actually had conversations with her son who 'died'.

* * *

Roger had also noticed while reading *Psychic World* that there was a group based in Scole, in Norfolk, called the NOAH'S ARK SOCIETY for physical mediumship. He arranged to join them at their next meeting in Norfolk, which was to be another demonstration of physical mediumship. I was all in favour of his going, as this sort of mediumship was rare and another source of interest for us. Roger describes briefly what happened:

"The demonstration was held in a cellar, in total darkness. The medium was tied to a chair (to avoid any cheating), and all the lights were turned off. Then, in the darkness, various luminous artefacts were seen whizzing around the room accompanied by the voices of incarnate beings, to which many of the people present replied, "Welcome friend". The purpose of all this was to replicate a style of mediumship that was apparently more common many years ago. I must say that it left me feeling rather bewildered, wondering what it was all about. I remember thinking, on my long drive back to Yorkshire, that what we had already witnessed from Steve seemed to be so much more relevant to people."

When Roger told me of his disappointment I felt let down too, as I thought that he would come back full of the wonders of physical mediumship. Instead he was rather bemused by the whole thing and the outcome was not what he had expected. For him, there was very little proof of survival. As physical mediumship is supposed to be the ultimate proof that one can receive of survival, we asked ourselves if it was worth continuing with our search as our friendship with Steve was answering more of our questions than anything else at the time. As Roger has mentioned, what Steve was doing was producing a more positive response from people, and we concluded that perhaps we should be satisfied with that alone.

CHAPTER 10

"How would you like to move down to Somerset?" Roger asked me one day. It was nearly three years since Lisa's passing and we had reached a level in our grief of quiet acceptance now, knowing that she hadn't left us but was still around with Steve, helping us to move on another pathway of our lives. He often reassured us that he felt she was with him, still standing back and not coming forward, and we believed him; if anyone should know it would be Steve. His sensitivity was proven time and again to be correct and we never doubted him; it calmed our feelings of despair in our loss.

Steve was now doing more demonstrations outside the churches. It was always exciting to watch him and we never tired of witnessing the joy on the faces of people seeing him for the first time as they received messages from their loved ones. We were also a bit envious, always hoping that Lisa might just step forward to say hello. We enjoyed helping him at these demonstrations and sometimes Caroline would come along to sit and listen. She was so used to his gift that she took it all in her stride!

I wanted to tell everyone that we met about Steve's extraordinary gift and how it had helped so many but, because of the adverse reaction that Spiritualism seemed to provoke in many people of different faiths, we both kept quiet. Steve was used to receiving negative reactions so it didn't seem to bother him too much, but from my point of view I resented not being able to speak out. The only time I did was when I was doing my bit of philosophy! I found it difficult to come to terms with the fact we have always been taught that we are all Spirit, with the Bible acknowledging this, and yet actually to try to prove that our spirit lives on is unacceptable! In fact some people in their ignorance call it wicked. This makes me feel angry, because if my daughter wanted to come through to a medium and tell me that she was fine and that she loved us how can that be called wicked? Steve had explained to us in our discussions on Sunday evenings that he could not demand anyone to come through to him, and that it was the spirit world that decided who would be allowed through to communicate.

Roger was still self-employed, and things hadn't been easy for him in his work. He had had feelings of restlessness for some time, so relocating wouldn't be a problem. I had spoken with my sister Ann, who lived in Somerset, a few weeks earlier and she had mentioned that her husband Allan would be moving out to Oman in the next few months. He had been working for the Omanis for a few years and now they had offered him long-term employment and it sounded like an offer he couldn't refuse. Ann would be staying behind at home until they could find a suitable person to rent their lovely old farmhouse and then she would fly out to join Allan.

I wasn't totally surprised at Roger's question as I had secretly been wondering whether it was an opportunity for us to take. "I would love to move down there," I replied. We had made several journeys down that way over the previous few years, ever since my parents had retired and had had a lovely bungalow built near Ann and Allan's home. Whenever we neared Somerset we always felt as if we were going home. It was a lovely, warm and welcoming sight to see the road sign saying 'Somerset'. We both loved Yorkshire and had spent many happy years there, but now we felt it was time to move on. I was feeling emotionally drained and Roger needed a complete break as he had been unable to settle down in his work since Lisa's death. Lisa's garden would be looked after by Lesley, who was now married with three children and lived not far away in the next village. It wouldn't be too much trouble for her just to take the short journey to do a bit of weeding, etc. I had looked after the little garden and it was always full of flowers and I was happy for Lesley to take it on in my place. I told myself that Lisa wasn't there anyway, for we both knew that she would be with us wherever we chose to be.

I phoned Ann immediately we had made the decision to go, and she greeted the news with joy: of course we could look after her home - far better that someone in the family would be looking after it rather than strangers. My parents, who were both disabled, had now moved into Ann's cottage as father's multiple sclerosis (MS) was worsening. They had converted one end of the Somerset longhouse into a lovely self-contained one-bedroom annex. It had originally been the storehouse for fruit and vegetables, as the previous owner had been a market gardener and had supplied the town with his home-grown produce. When they heard the news that we were moving down to look after the cottage while Allan and Ann were away, they were delighted.

We felt very sad that we were leaving Steve, but he also felt it was the right time and the right move, and that we would see each other again in the near future. I knew that Lisa would approve of our move to Somerset, as she had been down there several times to visit her gran and grandpa and loved it. There is always sadness at leaving memories behind, but we both felt we had to move on; this door had been opened for us and we knew we had to seize the chance.

Moving is exhausting work, and each time I swear it will be the last time. But, as with childbirth, we forget the pain and we have more children! This time, instead of looking for a buyer for our cottage, we decided to rent it out and it wasn't long before we had a couple wanting to move in almost immediately. We loved our little cottage - it had so many memories, good and sad - but a new life beckoned us in Somerset.

The van we rented was stacked to the roof each time we went down to Somerset. We had made the decision to do the removal ourselves as it would be cheaper. Never again! It took two journeys in quick succession and we were worn out with all the travelling, packing and unpacking. Rupert didn't know whether he was coming or going and neither did we! However, on our final journey, as we approached Somerset, we saw a lovely full moon over the Mendips and we sensed a deep feeling inside that we were coming home. Ann had moved a lot of her furniture around to make space for ours, but we still ended up putting some in storage in the barn. There was so much space in her cottage compared with the little home we had just left, with long passageways between the rooms, and the kitchen was in typical farmhouse style. One thing was for sure, we would have to get used to much more walking!

Once Ann had left to join Allan in Oman, we began the business of getting to know the quirks of living in someone else's house. For a start, there was the Rayburn. I had been used to a quick-response gas cooker, but the Rayburn was a completely different obstacle, and I never got used to it in all the time we were there. For one thing, because of the heavy iron door, I couldn't smell food cooking and I blackened many a chicken because I had forgotten it was cooking inside!

Rupert also had to get used to a different way of life. He had an acre of walled garden to wander around in and then there were the cats - long-time enemies of his. There were three cats and, needless to say, the ensuing weeks were devoted to keeping them and Rupert apart - not an easy job, but we managed somehow. Eventually, with much patience and firmness, Rupert gradually came around to the idea of having cats around; besides he was still missing Paddy, so my parent's tabby cat, Monty, became his best friend. Throughout his life, Rupert had disliked cats so much that on two occasions we had had to rescue the unfortunate victim from certain death and pay the vet's fees as compensation to the owner. He would just about tolerate our own cat, but certainly not a strange cat that happened to stray into our garden. Consequently, we were always on the lookout for the unexpected - something that became second nature to us.

Maybe it was Rupert's age that made him a bit more docile with Monty, or perhaps it was because Monty was a loner and didn't get on with Ann's cats that made them become firm friends. They would search for each other every morning and touch noses as a greeting, and then follow each other around the garden. It was a lovely friendship that would last for several years.

Life was certainly busy. There was an enormous garden to look after and Roger was preoccupied with setting up his business. Lisa was forever in our thoughts and we missed her terribly, as well as Steve's company and his demonstrations. Frances phoned every week and we made plans for her family to come down for their holidays, seeing as we now lived in a very convenient location! Frances spoke often of Lisa, but Lesley, on the few occasions that she contacted us, never mentioned her, preferring to talk of daily trivia; she was still remaining silent with her memories.

My parents were still fairly active, and although each had a walking disability it didn't stop them from going out in the car and lunching frequently at a pub along their journey into the countryside. Father was in his mid-70s and had a domineering personality that could be rather fearsome at times, while Mother's character is totally the opposite. She is a very gentle person, never wishing to cause any trouble to anyone, and everyone loves her; she is everyone's favourite granny.

Father frequently popped in to see us and have a chat, or rather a deep and meaningful discussion, something that Mother wasn't very good at. There was a passageway that led from their place to ours and the creaking door handle became a familiar sound, warning us that Father was on his way through!

A few months after we had moved, Roger and I decided to visit the Spiritualist church in Taunton. It was held in a community hall in a pleasant place just outside the town and we looked forward to meeting new people. We enjoyed the service until the medium started to demonstrate and it was then we realised how much we missed Steve's demonstrations. He was so accurate and sure of what he was hearing and the responses were so positive that anything less was not acceptable to us, and there were an awful lot of 'nos' that evening. We were introduced to several mediums following the service and after making polite conversation we agreed that we would go along again sometime, but we were not feeling particularly enthusiastic as we had been spoilt!

CHAPTER 11

I had asked Mother and Father round for supper and was busy in the kitchen preparing the meal. Tonight we would mention to them about our friend Steve and how we had been attending the Spiritualist churches over the last few years since Lisa had died. Father was always ready to have discussions, but we knew that sometimes these could lead to vehement arguments. We were determined to keep it 'low key' and not dwell too much on the subject, but I wanted them to know as it had helped us so much. Both of them had been devastated when Lisa died, as they had travelled to Bedford to see her being awarded her degree before going on to teach at The Central. They were so proud of her and she had a special place in their hearts being their youngest grandchild.

Father had been the treasurer at the little village church and was a regular attendee at the Sunday morning services since they had moved to Somerset. I think I would have labelled him religious, as he gave us the appearance of being a devout Christian and would take offence if I uttered "Oh God" in exasperation at something. Mother didn't believe in anything, she never discussed her thoughts on the subject and she didn't go to church with Father except on high days and holidays. It had been the same when Ann and I were in our early teens. I will always remember when he escorted us to Sunday School in his old gardening clothes, complete with Wellingtons, and left us at the door. I was so embarrassed! He very rarely went to church in those days, but as age crept on he decided it was better to be on the safe side, just in case it was held against him in the future I suppose. Mother never went, even though my grandfather had always been involved with the church and was a church warden for many years. She didn't believe in anything then, and still doesn't now.

The sound of the creaking handle as they came through the passageway announced their arrival. "Anybody there?" Father shouted. This was his usual greeting and one we were getting used to. "Come in," I shouted back.

I served out the dinner. We still hadn't mentioned Steve, and I was hoping the wine would be mellowing Father's temperament! "Have we mentioned to you about our friend Steve?" Roger said. "Steve, Steve - who's that?" enquired Father. There followed a short but detailed explanation of who Steve was, what he did, and how he had helped us over the last few years. There was an incredulous silence; personally I don't think Mother had understood anything that we had tried to explain, as there was a familiar blank look on her face. Father, to give him credit, appeared interested and started to ask probing questions. We felt as if we were being examined by the headmaster. Trying to answer his questions and trying to make sense of them was difficult. How can you explain to someone that has an unquestionable faith in God that you can actually communicate with a person that has died? It was a very spurious idea and certainly one that needed more thought. It was time to change the subject, but the seed had been planted. No doubt I would get the third degree at a later stage! We finished our meal, and Steve's name was not mentioned again throughout the rest of the evening.

By now, we were missing the atmosphere of Una's church and Steve's demonstrations. We could find nothing to replace them down there. "Do you think Steve would come down here to demonstrate?" Roger asked. "They wouldn't know what had hit them," I replied. Certainly we hadn't seen anybody that gave us the same enthusiasm as we had experienced with Steve's demonstrations in Yorkshire. I worried that I was being too fussy and expecting too much, but I quickly stopped thinking that way because I realised that it wasn't too much to expect, from somebody who calls him- or herself a medium, to hear proof of survival - after all, isn't that what mediumship is all about? The demonstrations that we had witnessed so far hadn't come up to the standard we expected; in fact, some of them were sadly lacking in proof of anything at all. It must put a lot of newcomers off going to a Spiritualist church if the standard is so low, I thought. If only they could see someone like Steve it would really give them something to think about.

I heard the sound of the door handle creaking as Father shuffled his way through the passageway. He walked with a distinctive dragging of the feet as his legs were very weak. He had been invalided out of the army in 1945 and the MS had been a very slow progression over the years. However, he was one of the lucky people, because he was still able to walk even if it was with two sticks. He had an iron will and had fought against the weakness in his legs, refusing to give in. Unfortunately, this had the effect of producing extreme tiredness and his already short temper became even shorter. Mother consequently had a very difficult time with him. Ann and I were raised in a family dominated by Father, as

Mother didn't have the strength of character to stand up for her own views, and as children we had to obey his word or the consequences weren't worth the lectures that followed. As far as we were all concerned his word was law.

Father came into the kitchen and sat down. Roger was working in the office upstairs and I was wishing that he would come down and make an appearance, as my instinct told me I was going to need some support.

"So who is this Steve?" Father asked.

"He is a friend who has been a great support to us since Lisa died," I replied, reasonably patiently.

Our previous conversation with Mother and Father had obviously been on his mind, and when something bothers Father he is like a terrier with a rat, he will not let go!

"But he hears voices," was the retort.

"Yes, they are from our loved ones who have gone on before," I explained. I was finding it more difficult to sound plausible as Father was staring at me with narrowed eyes, a trick that he often used to try to intimidate people who he felt were trying to outwit him. "Steve is clairaudient, and he has an amazing gift that helps people who have been bereaved. He has certainly helped us," I continued, wanting to end the conversation as Father was beginning to unnerve me.

"Where is this Steve? Is he coming down here?"

"Roger is going to ask him if he could find the time. He is very busy and much in demand."

"Well, I would like to meet this Steve," Father said, as he manoeuvred himself out of the chair and made for the door.

"Fine, we will introduce you," I responded to the closing door.

And that was it, for the time being at least! Why, oh why, did I always feel so ill at ease in his company? Here was I, a grown woman, and I still felt like a small child in Father's presence! Roger had heard some of the conversation as he came downstairs, but he had quickly retreated thinking he was best out of it, the coward - but this was the beginning of the effect that Father had on all of us.

The response from Steve, on being asked if he would consider coming down to the West Country to work, was really positive. It was proposed that he could stay with us and, to begin with, as an introduction to the people of the south-west, he could work in some of the churches in Somerset and Devon. We felt it would be an ideal place for him to come and relax as well as to demonstrate to a new audience. We couldn't wait to see him again!

When Ann and Allan left their cottage to live out in Oman, they left Roger and I in charge, and this included looking after not only the aforementioned cats, but also the goats, and keeping their enormous but beautiful walled garden under control. Luckily, I enjoyed gardening and had tended an allotment in Yorkshire, so growing my own vegetables wasn't a hardship. In fact the allotment was situated just over the wall from Lisa's garden in the churchyard and I had always felt close to her when I was working there. Roger has never been keen on gardening but does enjoy the fruits of my labours, although he will sometimes offer to do any heavier work for me.

Father took a very keen interest in my endeavours and often came out to have a chat while I was working. Their conservatory overlooked the vegetable garden, which meant there was little privacy for me to potter around. It had been some years since Father had been able to do anything in the garden and he would often reward my efforts with criticism. He was a perfectionist and had created beautiful gardens when he had been able to move around more easily, so it must have been very frustrating for him simply to watch me because he couldn't do it himself. But I wished on more than one occasion that he would just leave me alone and let me get on with it in my own way.

Roger had been busy making arrangements with various churches in Devon where Steve would be working. He was due to come down shortly and his first demonstration was to be at Paignton Spiritualist Church. It could hold two hundred people, and tickets had sold out within a few days of their going on sale, news having travelled fast about the gifted young medium!

Steve's arrival was greeted with enthusiasm by us both and he quickly made himself at home. Caroline stayed in Yorkshire, and was quite used to keeping things going whilst Steve was away, knowing how important his work was to him. So that she didn't think she had been forgotten, we sent her a bouquet of flowers to thank her for letting Steve come down. We were so happy he was here at last!

CHAPTER 12

As promised, we introduced Steve to Father and they both sat in our kitchen having a pleasant chat. Everything seemed to be going well, Father was taking an interest in what Steve had to say and eventually Father said goodbye and made his way back through the passageway. Mother hadn't bothered to come and say hello - she had obviously decided to let Father sound Steve out and report back to her. She wasn't being rude, but it was always Father that led the way in their marriage and she would go along with whatever he said. How different from today's society where the women are treated as equals and are not afraid to speak up for themselves.

The following evening we made the journey down to Paignton, which presented a lovely drive through the Devon countryside. We eventually found the church situated on a main road with a long queue of people outside, and Steve couldn't believe they were all waiting for him! We felt quite excited at the prospect of Steve's first demonstration in Devon, and it was obvious from the atmosphere in the church that everyone was feeling the same! We received a welcome cup of tea and chatted with the organisers, who asked whether Roger and I would mind sitting up on the rostrum with Steve as the church was so full and there weren't any more spare seats available. In fact it was an ideal place to observe the reactions of the people who received messages and since then we have always sat on the rostrum!

It is fascinating to watch Steve work at such close quarters. He is confined to a space much smaller than a stage and his energy while giving out messages has to be limited to either stamping his foot or banging his fist on the surrounding edge of the rostrum to emphasise a point!

It was around this time that Steve experienced a physical change in his mediumship. His left hand began to take on a tight, curled appearance, and the colour was often tinged with blue. Apparently this was a guide called Archie, who had a deformed hand while on earth, and he was showing his presence to Steve whilst he was demonstrating. At that time Steve knew very little about Archie, but he found comfort in his presence as he knew that Spirit were with him and would be there to give him guidance. After the demonstration his hand would unfurl and give no discomfort even though it had been held like that for over an hour. I defy anyone to try to hold that position intentionally for that length of time without it causing pain.

That first evening at Paignton was a huge success. It was the first time that many had seen anyone like Steve, who was so natural with his gift and had his own unique way of giving out their messages. Everyone wanted Steve back again and Roger was glad to be able to arrange a date for a future visit. We knew that Steve would be appreciated down there as, firstly, he has such a rare and wonderful gift and, secondly, he is sincere and has such a natural warmth with people. He is very down to earth and has an ability to put people at ease when speaking with them whilst delivering a message from a loved one. We now visit Paignton every year, with Steve commanding a full house each time, as tickets sell out within days of going on sale.

On the long drive home, we ordered chicken kebabs as we were all ravenous, especially Steve. His appetite is legendary and it would be usual for him to have an extra large kebab together with a double helping of chips and an extra large salad with extra garlic sauce - he was a tired and hungry man after giving out so much energy on behalf of the Spirit world!

Roger had been busy arranging other church venues and, as I had predicted, they didn't know what had hit them! We had a marvellous first week visiting many Devon areas that Steve hadn't been to before, and we received a warm reception from everyone, all eager for him to return as soon as possible. Steve returned home to Caroline after a week away and Roger and I spent the next few days recovering, as Steve's energy was something to which we had become unaccustomed - both of us were used to a quiet life down in the West Country!

* * *

Sometimes it was necessary for Roger to work away from the cottage. Although he had his office at home, a visit to his head office was occasionally necessary. It was while he was out that I decided to tackle the vegetable garden - not a small undertaking and I expected it to take at least most of the morning as it was not the average-sized garden! I settled Rupert down on the path. His eyesight was failing and old age had caught up with him so he very rarely left my side. Random thoughts were going through my head whilst I was busy hoeing at the abundance of weeds, when I heard the familiar sound of the conservatory door opening and Father walked slowly down the path towards me. I am not stopping now, as I have just started, I thought.

"I have been giving some thought to what this Steve does," he began. "I don't agree with it, hearing voices. What does he mean he hears voices? One must have faith. You do not have faith. You are no daughter of mine!" he began to shout.

I stood up and looked at him. I was speechless. But before I could think of an answer, he shouted at me, "You must have faith!" He almost spat the word at me. "I don't want him down here again. The atmosphere in this cottage is lowered when he comes down."

I could not believe what I was hearing. My Father was dictating that Steve shouldn't come down to see us again - who did he think he was? But I knew the answer. Father wanted to be in control. We had come down to look after Allan and Ann's cottage while they were away, and because Father had been living there for nearly twenty years he felt he should be the one in charge! Unfortunately, because both he and Mother were disabled this was not possible. Besides, we were also responsible for looking after our nephew who had started boarding school and we had been left with the understanding that it was our responsibility to see that everything ran smoothly during my sister's absence. But Father had always been the one in control of his family and because of his age and disability he was losing the one thing that made him feel important.

"It is none of your business who we invite down here. Steve is our friend and he will be coming down here again."

I had started to shout, trying to catch his attention, but he wasn't going to - and didn't want to - hear what I had to say. Over and over again, he shouted that I hadn't any faith and that I was no daughter of his. His face had turned a shade of red, he was so very, very angry. After several minutes he started walking away and I watched him struggle along the path with his awkward shuffle and then disappear inside, banging the door behind him. I felt deeply hurt that he was unable to approach the subject of Steve without feeling this deep anger and having to resort to shouting. I also felt helpless at not being allowed to have my say. He wasn't interested in my side of the argument.

I didn't feel like continuing with the garden, so I led Rupert back indoors and then the tears came - tears of anger and frustration. How could this eighty-year-old man have such an effect on me? But it had always been the same: if any member of the family disagreed with him it would end in a shouting match until he wore us down and he got his own way. It was all very well talking about faith, but even if you have faith does that make you a better person than anyone else?

Roger returned home and I told him all about the unsavoury episode with Father. I was glad that Roger hadn't been at home at the time because I know that he would have been very hurt by Father's attitude. If it hadn't been for Steve I don't know how we would have coped with Lisa's death, as there had been many black, despairing days when we had almost given up. When we had previously explained to Father how Steve had helped us, he had seemed to accept what was said, but now he had shown us how he really felt; that he was deeply disturbed by Steve's gift. He clearly did not wish to discuss it further and was obviously one of those ignorant people who thought it evil.

In the days that followed there was an uneasy atmosphere

with Father. His attitude towards us was unforgiving and Mother kept trying to make peace by telling us not to take any notice. This had always been her bolt-hole: if there had been trouble between them, she would ignore what was being said and quietly go about her business. But we couldn't do that, because Steve was coming down again in the near future and we had to work out how we were going to survive the week he was here, with Father just next door!

However, I had more important things on my mind at that time. Rupert was becoming more dependent on us for help; in fact he was getting a bit senile. We often had to let him out at night and he would stand and stare into the distance, having forgotten what he was supposed to be doing. He would stand for a long time and we had to coax him into action just so that we could get back to bed. It was getting more obvious that he was finding life very difficult and we decided to seek advice from our vet. Rupert was a rescue dog and had been with us since he was seven weeks old and now, at the ripe old age of fifteen, his back legs were weak and he was having difficulty supporting himself. We loved him dearly, as he had been such a loyal and loving dog all these years, and when the vet said that his time had come we agreed that Rupert should be at home with us holding him as we had done for Paddy. Again I said a little prayer to Lisa, asking her to take him and to look after him as she would have done for Paddy. Our hearts were heavy and the tears flowed once again, but we knew that Rupert would be with his old friend, and that now Lisa had all of our pets to keep her company! Monty missed Rupert very much and in the days that followed he came looking for him whenever I appeared in the garden. It was so sad to see, but within a few weeks he had settled down to being on his own once more, and Rupert is now buried under a beautiful copper beech in the paddock.

We loved living in the old farmhouse with its beautiful garden and surrounding paddocks; we felt at peace. Lisa had always loved the house and garden and she would have approved of the fact that we were there. We knew we had made the right move. Although we missed Yorkshire with its moors and hills, we had exchanged them for the gentle, rolling hills of Somerset and Devon that were on our doorstep.

We were also excited about introducing Steve to new people, who didn't go to a Spiritualist church, at bigger public venues. The first week we had organised, with Steve demonstrating at the churches, was such a success that Roger booked our first big venue, Plymouth Guildhall. Having spoken with Steve on the phone and explained about the trouble we were having with Father, he said, "Not to worry, he won't know that I'm there." He was so used to ignorance about his work and the nasty remarks that some people made that it was like water off a duck's back! He was far more concerned for us and how we were feeling about it.

Steve arrived a couple of weeks later. He parked his car in the yard and nipped around to the back door. "I'm so sorry you have to creep around like this," I apologised, feeling guilty that he should have to keep a low profile. I am sure readers will think that Steve shouldn't have had to be so furtive, but if you had known my Father then I am certain that you would have wanted to keep the peace just like me! We had to live there for the next few years and it just wasn't worth the unpleasantness, so if Steve could move around but be invisible to Father, then it was certainly worth it for our sake! If we heard the sound of the creaking door handle and the familiar shuffling of his walk, Steve would rush upstairs and stay out of sight until Father had departed. If Steve wanted to go out, we would peer around the corner of the house to make sure the coast was clear and then he would quickly get into his car and make a hasty retreat! When walking around the garden, Steve would take the path furthest away from my parents' house, but as there were plenty of trees around this didn't cause too much of a problem. And so it went on like this for several years, whenever Steve stayed with us.

CHAPTER 13

We had sold all the tickets for the Plymouth Guildhall, and as we travelled down on the evening of the demonstration we discussed the possibility of other venues that could be arranged as it had become obvious that Steve was much in demand. At that time Steve was still working at the churches in the south-west, but he really wanted to reach new people, so larger venues for those that didn't attend Spiritualist churches were the obvious answer. We arrived outside the Guildhall rather early and to our amazement a queue of people stretching down the street was already waiting! The caretaker greeted us as we hurried inside and closed the doors behind us; we needed to make sure that everything was in place before letting anyone inside.

"Shall I let them in?" the caretaker asked. "Yes, I'm ready, but there won't be much to do as we have sold all the tickets," I replied. Little did I know that the next half an hour was going to be harrowing. Roger had come up to give me some help if I needed it, and thank goodness he did because as the doors opened the people surged in - but they didn't have tickets, they were expecting to pay on the door. The advert in the paper had been printed that day and had said "pay on the door"; unfortunately, the paper had put it in by mistake and we had already sold out! We let those who had tickets through to the hall, and had to tell the others who had come expecting to pay that there had been a mistake in the paper. That was when the atmosphere changed, and although Roger was extremely apologetic and tried to explain it wasn't our fault some people started to shout at him. That was when the caretaker took over and told Roger to get back inside for his own safety. Those with tickets filed in quickly and the hall was soon filled to capacity. We shut the doors, leaving an angry crowd outside. Watching through the windows we heard the mutterings from those that were left and felt sorry for the ones that had come some distance, but it hadn't been our fault that so many were disappointed - it was a genuine mistake by the paper.

The evening was a resounding success, Steve had made a big impression at Plymouth and we announced that he would be back again soon. Seeing all the smiling faces as the people were leaving and the genuine interest from many, a thought flashed through my mind. If only Father had been able to see the effect that Steve had on these people, I am sure he would have been amazed.

We wanted to say goodnight to people as they left, so we all waited by the door. We could hear a group of people chatting outside, rather excitedly. One lady came up to Steve and asked if she could touch his arm. It was a lady to whom Steve had given a message during the evening, from her mother. During the message he had asked her to touch his arm - which she did. The lady then turned to her friends and said, "It was, you know. It was mum's arm that I felt during the message, not Steve's."

It was quite a long drive home and Steve was tired and hungry but also elated that the evening had been such a success. We knew that the south-west was going to be a good area in which to plan more of these public demonstrations, and as we drew nearer to home the obligatory phone call to Mr Scrumptious was made!

* * *

Steve had been booked to work at several of the churches in Devon. Occasionally we had to stay away for a night and then we all booked into a bed and breakfast place. This happened when we stayed at Bude, as Steve was working in the town's Spiritualist church. The house we stayed in was run by two sisters, Joan and Eileen. They were kindness itself, and we were looked after so well, especially Steve, who was thoroughly spoilt! I don't think he will ever forget Joan bringing his early morning tea wearing her rather short nightie! She was the president of the church and was so happy to have Steve do a demonstration as it helped to bring new people into the congregation. There was a lot of laughter and fun when we stayed there and the memories will always stay with us!

At home, Father had no idea that Steve was around. If any mention was made of the extra car, we said that it was because we had some friends to stay. The atmosphere was still uneasy though. I was always on my guard in case the subject of Steve came up again. Because we lived under the same roof, albeit in separate accommodation, and my parents needed our help due to their disabilities, it was inevitable that our paths would cross most days.

* * *

We were back to our usual routine as Steve had now returned to Yorkshire and Caroline and again the house seemed very quiet. I popped into 'next door' and asked if there was any shopping they would like me to do. Father sat at the table, head in hands, a sign that he was feeling very depressed. Mother was busying herself in the kitchen and so I addressed my question to Father.

"Sit down," he said, so I sat at the table waiting for what I thought was going to be the inevitable same old story. "I want to be buried not cremated," he said. "I don't think I have long to go."

"If that's what you want," I replied.

"Buried," he emphasised.

"Okay, but why buried in particular?" I asked.

"Because that is the way one should be. I believe that you lie in the grave for three days and then your spirit rises up."

Well, you can imagine my reaction! "You really believe that you will lie in the grave for three days and then you are allowed to go to heaven?" I responded a bit facetiously.

But Father was deadly serious, and in the absence of a reply I took the opportunity to have my say! "But your spirit leaves your body when you die and then you go to whatever place you have made for yourself on this earth."

"I think you're wrong. You lie in the grave for three days and then your spirit rises up and, yes, you take your place in heaven, so I want you to make sure that I am buried and not cremated."

I reassured him that I would take care of his wishes when he died. I approached Mother in the kitchen and asked her if she would like to be buried with Father. Her reaction surprised me as she firmly said no, she did not want to be buried with him and anyway she didn't believe in any of it! What she was referring to I'm not sure but I didn't have a chance to find out because the phone rang at that moment so I left them both, still not knowing if they required any shopping. Never mind, I would sort that out later. I was thinking over what Father had just said about his spirit being in the grave for three days. I know that he was referring to the resurrection of Jesus and the Bible says that after three days he was risen again. But the whole concept seemed so strange because in hot countries the body is cremated within hours of death, so what happens to the spirit then? Does it hang around for three days somewhere? I decided to ask Steve what he thought about the whole idea of the spirit waiting for three days before being resurrected. "But I can't see the point," was the reply. "Nor can I. It just doesn't make sense," I said. I reminded myself to mention to Father that he would be probably be lying in the chapel of rest for three days anyway before he was buried, so he might have a bit longer to wait than three days before he went to heaven! But I kept my thoughts to myself so as not to provoke another argument.

Despite all the demonstrations we had attended we still hadn't received a message from Lisa and I was thinking that perhaps it wasn't meant to be. Steve has always said that he is aware that she is around while he is demonstrating but still standing at the back of him and not coming forward. It was a bit of a surprise, however, when Steve told us that when he was having a bath he had caught a glimpse of Lisa watching him from the corner of the bathroom. He found it quite amusing that she was there: what did she find interesting, I wonder?!

There was one occasion at Paignton when we were sitting not on the rostrum but this time on the back-row seats when

Steve mentioned that he wanted to speak with someone who was wearing a mauve dress. He went on to give a date and I could answer yes to his questions, but did I put my hand up? No, instead I kept my hands in my lap as I felt people would think it was all 'fixed'. So much for our telling everyone else to put their hands up immediately they think Steve is talking to them. The lady he was addressing was not responding positively, in fact she seemed quite confused, so the message may have been for me and due to my stupidity I missed my chance - since then I have resolved to be more positive!

Another church was in Bideford, and the demonstration was held in an old hall with a healing room downstairs where we used to gather before and after the service. It wasn't a large place so the numbers were limited and Steve was more than happy to work there to help boost the congregation. He had just finished another successful demonstration, giving out some lovely messages for many people, and was sitting chatting with us in the healing room, when ... but Roger can relate the rest of the story:

"Steve turned to me and said, quite out of the blue, 'What's the web I am seeing? It's like a spider's web with everything connected.' (Steve was at that time neither technically minded nor computer literate, and he always used to tell us that the most technical he ever got was when he turned his mobile phone on - and he found that difficult too!) He had no idea of the web being associated with computers; in fact it wasn't a very familiar concept to us as we only used our computer for my work.

Now I had been considering, in my own mind at least, that it would be great if Steve had his own website one day, but I didn't have any contacts. As we were leaving, I happened to mention this to the president of the church, and she said to me, 'Why don't you contact Mark, he's a web designer.' I could not believe the coincidence (although I was beginning to by now - maybe I'm a bit slow!) Anyway, she gave me a contact number, which I followed up a few days later. After several meetings with Mark to discuss formats, etc., we then let the expert take over and in 1999 Steve had his first website." There were a lot of hiccups to begin with as Roger and I had a lot to learn! It was thrilling to have contact with so many people who had been to see Steve and wanted to let us know how much he had helped them. But that was only the beginning. Little did we realise how much it was going to expand!

CHAPTER 14

Steve had been coming down to us twice a year and we had been busy finding new public venues for him. He was leading a hectic life in Yorkshire, combining his hairdressing business with his spiritual work and also looking after his growing family, but his energy never seemed to tire and we were amazed at what he packed into his life. Unfortunately he was still having to avoid Father on his visits to us, so there was a lot of creeping around. One time when Father came through the passageway, Steve was on his phone upstairs and, as many of you will know, Steve has rather a loud voice. He was chatting away to a friend, completely oblivious to Father's presence downstairs, and I was frantically trying to cover up Steve's voice by speaking loudly as Father was a bit deaf anyway! I sat him down in the kitchen, closing the door and praying that Steve wouldn't come bounding down the stairs as he usually did. Luckily he must have heard me talking to Father before he burst into the kitchen and tactfully disappeared into another room! Yes, at times it was difficult, but it didn't really worry us too much so long as we were careful. There was no way I was going to let myself be subjected to another of Father's outbursts. Ann and I have always regretted that we were never able to have a closer relationship with Father, but my sister was always a bit afraid of him and I would rather avoid him for fear of any confrontation. He enjoyed arguments and seemed to thrive on them trying to win a point every time, Steve said that it was probably the only thing that kept him going!

Our time at the lovely old farmhouse was almost up - Ann and Allan were coming home from Oman the following year for good, as Allan had reached retirement. This meant that Roger and I had to find somewhere nearby to live as Ann had already mentioned to us that she didn't want us to go far away as she didn't think she could cope with two disabled people who were getting more dependent on our help.

When Allan and Ann came home on their holidays from Oman they used to go with us to see other mediums who were demonstrating in the area. They had already seen Steve work and so they were interested in seeing what others had to offer. It was on one of these evenings that we decided to go into Taunton and watch a medium work on stage at our local theatre. We could not believe what we were hearing as, besides a great number of 'nos', there was a certain amount of aggression if the messages weren't accepted. It was almost a case of 'You will believe what I'm saying. Don't contradict me!' I'm afraid we all felt rather embarrassed by the whole affair and took ourselves off to the pub for the rest of the evening. That example of mediumship was not what I wanted to share with family or friends, it didn't feel right, and we did notice that several others also left during the interval.

On another occasion just Ann and I went to watch a medium who was working locally, and as we sat there listening he suddenly turned to me and said, "You make good Yorkshire puddings." It was only a small gathering that night, crowded into the local Quaker Hall sitting in half-circles. I had met the medium a few months before and it was then that he mentioned he was coming down our way and asked if we would like to go and see him work. Of course I said yes, as we were interested to see anyone who might possibly come up to the standard we now expected from any medium. Now that he was addressing me, I found that I was instantly paying more attention, as I must admit I had switched off somewhat having found it rather boring. However, my expertise at Yorkshire puddings was not what I had expected to hear about, and I tried to associate this with proof of survival to no avail, but I acknowledged the fact and waited to hear more. However, it seemed his guide got in the way and was being rather mischievous (apparently it was a young boy) and the message deviated to a story of how this young boy created mayhem around him. That was the end of my so-called message and the evening, as far as we were both concerned, was again another disappointment. In all our subsequent searching for someone who could come up to Steve's standard, there has been no one about whom, with hands on our hearts, we could say, "Yes, he/she is as good as Steve." We appreciate that everyone has their own particular style of delivering messages, but the responses from the audience should always be positive and so far we had encountered a lot of negativity.

During the week, Father had fallen in the house and had suffered a lot of pain, necessitating the assistance of the District Nurse who was calling in every day. It was obvious that age was catching up with both of my parents and their disabilities didn't help matters. Living 'out in the sticks' is not the best idea when you are old and a long way from the shops, and the idea of living in sheltered accommodation was not acceptable to Father, so there was no alternative solution but to 'soldier on' as he put it. Mother really didn't have any say in the matter, although secretly she would have liked to live nearer the town, being quite a sociable person who enjoyed the company of others. They were two complete opposites and had been married for over fifty years, but now in their old age they had grown apart, which was sad to see. With Ann and Allan finally coming back home they now had something else to focus on and were looking forward to their return.

Allan attended our little village church whenever possible, but he also found what Steve did amazing and has had long conversations about how it all works - not that Steve knows exactly what's going on! Allan is open minded about it all, which is a good thing as none of us knows all the answers and it would be arrogant of us to think we do. Today's young people have been educated to question and discuss topics in a way that in bygone years would not have been tolerated and we find many young people in the Spiritualist church who come to enjoy good mediumship and also question. They come to Steve's demonstrations and are able to have a quiet word with him afterwards, as he has always made time for those who need to speak with him.

There are some people that are frightened by the idea that we continue our lives on a different vibration. Maybe they suddenly realise that they will be accountable for the life they live here and how they have chosen to live it. Because this idea is frightening to them they choose to deny Steve's gift. This is, I am sure, why Father was so vehement about Steve's gift, as he had told all the family that he had failed very badly in his life, but as he never expanded on any details we were left to guess at what he had done specifically that was so bad!

We had been looking around for somewhere else to live and, as luck would have it (or was it fate?), Roger and I had found a lovely farm cottage just a mile away. The poor garden had been badly neglected and needed a lot of TLC; the good thing was that it was a manageable size and overlooked fields. Being situated on a farm, the only neighbours were sheep and cows in the field surrounding the farm cottage and, of course, the main house where the farmers lived. We had known the family for some years and it really was fortuitous for us to find that it was available but, as Steve said, it was meant to be! The next few months we were busy packing up and trying to organise our move to coincide with the return of Allan and Ann, and eventually we moved into our little cottage with the steep narrow stairs - so narrow that the bedroom furniture had to go through the landing window!

Over the following few months Roger looked for new venues for Steve and unfortunately some of the churches didn't respond very well to the news that Steve would now be doing public demonstrations. We have never been interested in the politics of the churches, as we have always been of the opinion that Steve's gift should be there for all and not just a few. They wanted to keep Steve for themselves, but his policy has always been to reach as many new people as possible and this would only be attainable through public demonstrations. Yet other churches welcomed the idea, as their view was that it would help bring more people into their church and this over the years has proved to be correct. While organising the public demonstrations we have always tried to include the churches and felt that it was right we should do so; after all, Steve's gift is given to him by Spirit and a church is a place in which we could also thank God for Steve's work. It was a big sadness to us that politics had to play any part in where Steve should be demonstrating, but he is a free spirit and will always have the last word on where he works and whatever he decides to do we will support him.

Steve came down to stay in our little cottage for the first time for his week's visit. He and Ann would trawl the second-hand shops in Taunton and he would come back laden with toys for the children and presents for us - he was always so pleased with all the bargains he had purchased! If it was a sunny day, he would sit in the garden doing his paperwork and make his phone calls - any excuse to top up his tan! On one shopping trip he came back with a jar of black olives, which he devoured whilst sitting in the garden, and then rubbed the olive oil all over himself to help enhance his tan! It's a memory we will never let him forget!

We had been down to Paignton church for a demonstration and Roger was driving us back home with Steve half asleep in the passenger seat.

Out of the blue, he suddenly said to Roger, "£60,000, what's £60,000?"

"I don't know Steve. I wish I did!"

"I'm being told £60,000." Steve couldn't say exactly who was telling him, but he said that whoever it was had a birthday in November.

Roger then asked him, "Why is that relevant Steve?"

Steve replied, "If I said that Lisa was telling me, you wouldn't believe me!"

Roger responded, "Well, Lisa's birthday is in November."

Steve was so surprised as he had no idea when her birthday was. We had never mentioned it because, as usual, we had hoped that one day we might just get a message and some things we had resolved never to tell him. It was a passing remark, but we were so used to Steve suddenly saying things that didn't make much sense to us that we just carried on talking.

On another occasion, coming back from Plymouth, Steve said to Roger, "Maureen has just told me that you should be working." Now Maureen was one of the mediums that we had met in the early days of our attending Una's church and she had told Roger that he should be healing. So we presumed that by 'working' she was now saying to Steve that Roger should be using his gift of healing. In fact, Roger had the opportunity to use his gift when one day we received a phone call from a lady who was distraught. Her beloved retriever could hardly move with its arthritis and she had been told by a friend that Roger might be able to give some healing, so please could she bring 'Bonnie' along? This lady was terribly upset as the vet had told her that there was nothing more he could do for 'Bonnie'. Of course Roger siad 'Yes' and see arrived within the hour, we had been so surprised to receive the call and could not think who migh have mentioned about Roger's healing hands.

When the lady arrived with Bonnie, it became obvious to us as she came through the door that 'Bonnie' was in pain and had difficulty walking. Roger sat them both in the quiet of the sitting room, while I busied myself in the kitchen. I thought I had better send a few thoughts out for help as it had been some time since Roger had used his gift!

For the next half hour Roger gave Bonnie some healing,

laying his hands over Bonnie, just as he had done for Paddy a few years before. The lady was so greatful for Roger's time, and when she left we asked her to keep in touch to let us know how 'Bonnie' fared in the next few days. The following week Roger received a lovely card to say that 'Bonnie' for the first time in months actually bounded down her drive when she got home and she couldn't thank him enough for his healing. We didn't hear anything more from her but I do hope that 'Bonnie' had another few years with her adoring mistress but we never found out who had mentioned to her about Roger's healing hands!

I have often asked Roger for healing when I have the usual aches and pains from arthritis and he has felt the familiar tingling in his hands when placing them over my aching back. I don't presume it to be a coincidence these days because the healing has relieved the aches and pains on more than a few occasions. One day Roger may be able to work more for other people with his healing hands, but until then I shall continue to make use of his gift!

CHAPTER 15

Roger had been having trouble with his eyes, the usual redness of an infection he thought, and he decided to visit the doctor. She, in her wisdom, said he should go to the hospital to see the eye consultant as it was a recurring problem, and she duly made the appointment. The visit to the hospital and the consultant led to Roger being given a scan and the results showed that he had MS. Luckily, the consultant told him, if you had to have MS, this was the type that was the least aggressive. His work as a financial adviser would be too stressful for him to continue due to the amount of driving it involved and the pressure of the work. He had been feeling very tired lately and one of the symptoms of MS is fatigue.

I naturally phoned Frances to tell her the news of Roger's diagnosis and how it was going to affect our lives, as things would have to change. I was in the middle of saying this when she suddenly asked, "Have you got a critical illness policy?" "I don't know," I replied. "I will mention it to Roger when he comes home." When I asked him later that evening he looked at me and said that he hadn't even thought about it, but yes he did have one. He hunted it out from amongst all his documents and then turned to me and said, "Guess what, it's for £60,000!"

We phoned Steve to tell him the good news. He remembered the conversation in the car a couple of months earlier, but we hadn't told him anything at that time about

Roger's visits to the hospital or about his impending scan. He was amazed at our good news. Again Steve had told us of something that was going to happen, but again we hadn't really taken it in. It is the same when people are given a message about twins coming in the family or asking if someone is expecting. Neither of these messages makes sense to the person at the time, but it usually comes to pass in the not too distant future! This must surely mean that our paths in life are already laid down and Steve occasionally is able to glimpse, or is actually told, what is likely to happen. We had been waiting for years to have a message or something tangible, but Lisa had chosen to speak to Steve in the privacy of our car, and then we just passed it off as wishful thinking! We should by now know better, because it was fifteen years ago that Steve told us we would be working for Spirit and we had denied it.

* * *

Since we have been living in Somerset, Roger has arranged many public demonstrations for Steve and he had thought for some time how marvellous it would be if everyone who received a message could hear it played back to them again when they got home. Steve speaks so quickly while working that many people forget what he has actually said and so a disk that recorded the evening would be ideal! We had bought a sound system a few years previously and now the next logical step was to record the evenings. After a few hiccups and much research, Roger now records every demonstration we attend. It is time consuming but well worth it, as we are told time and again how grateful people are for being able to listen again to their message, and they say it is also useful as they are able to play it to other members of the family who are a bit sceptical!

I would also just like to mention an incident that happened at one of the demonstrations we were organising. I had put out on the nearby tables half a dozen pieces of A4 paper, which were the phone lists, on which people can write down their name and telephone number so that I can give them a ring and remind them of the date that Steve is coming back to give a demonstration. I was standing nearby, watching as names and numbers were being written down at the end of the evening, when I heard a lady exclaim loudly to her friend that she certainly wouldn't be putting her name down as that was how they did the research on people! I wasn't able to reply as she disappeared with the crowd but I thought, if she only knew - I lead a busy life and to do any research on hundreds of names is quite honestly beyond my capability! It is simply another service that we offer to those who are interested in attending again and, considering that I speak with hundreds, such research just wouldn't be humanly possible. All I can assume is that that particular lady was a bit stunned at the accuracy of Steve's messages that evening and so we must have done some research, and that was the only answer she could come up with! Another lady that I spoke with on the telephone said that she was ordering a couple of tickets, really for her neighbour whom she felt needed some help. "I don't believe in any of this stuff," she said, "but my neighbour might find some comfort and so I will take her along." "That's a nice gesture," I replied, a bit taken aback because if she didn't really believe in any of 'this stuff' then why bother to take her neighbour to something she didn't believe in! I must admit I hoped she got the shock of her life and received a message herself, as well as her neighbour!

It was while we were at the Newport demonstration that I received a call from my sister to say that Father was very ill. Roger and I were staying at the hotel where the demonstration was being held, as it was too far to drive home that night. Father had been in a nursing home for the last year, and on each occasion we visited we saw his body become increasingly frail while his memory became worse. He still recognised us but could never remember our being there with him. Mother was never very keen to visit him as she didn't like the thought that perhaps one day she might also be a resident. "It will kill me," she always said but, being a more robust person, I don't think she will end up in a nursing home! On the occasions she visited Father she reluctantly held his hand as they sat together, not speaking but waiting until the nurse brought in a welcome cup of tea, at which point Mother would hurriedly withdraw her hand in relief. Father had relapses of health and more than once we received a call saying that we ought to go and see him before it was too late. On these occasions he was sleeping deeply and looking very ill - as though he wouldn't last the night - but by the next morning, to the astonishment of all the staff, he was sitting up demanding breakfast!

I was in our hotel room when the call came. The doctor was there with him as he was in much pain and she said to my sister she would give him an injection to calm him down. I had been told previously that if you talk to a person who is dying they can hear and can be comforted by your words and this I had mentioned to my sister. Steve had often given a message to someone saying that their words had been heard by the dead person, or even if they received a kiss or had their hand held, they had known about it. So Ann sat with Father and reassured him and told him that Mother would be all right, as we would look after her, and that there was really nothing to worry about and it was time for him to let go. I waited by the telephone in our room for further news when she phoned me a short time later to tell me what she had said and again shortly afterwards to say he had given up his fight. We both hoped he had heard Ann's comforting words and died peacefully.

I returned to the back of the hall to watch Steve giving out his messages and I wondered if Father would ever come back to me and just let me know that, yes, everything was all right and he was fine and also that he hadn't bothered to wait in the grave for three days! I wished desperately that I could have been with him, to tell him that he would see his mother and father and all his friends who had gone on before and that he would also see Lisa again. I also wished that we could have talked about what we had learnt since Lisa had died and I could have assured him that there was no fear in death but that he would be reborn and able to walk again, and be whole. I truly believe, because it makes sense to me, that there is no hell, but it is our own guilty conscience of the life we have led that faces us when we pass over; and that our life here is a lesson for our soul and the more we learn to give love and work for the benefit of others the higher the place that we shall attain in the next world.

* * *

Working with Steve is hectic (and we know that he won't mind us saying this), but we can't think of anything more enjoyable. We love meeting the hundreds of people who are so eager to go to his demonstrations, and also talking with many of them on the telephone. We travel all over the West Country and are constantly looking for new venues to organise, but Steve is only human and can only do so much physically. However, we have been able to introduce him down our way, and from the many emails we receive from people who have received messages from their loved ones, and who are so grateful for the hope that Steve has brought them, we know that our paths are going in the right direction.

Over the years I have been asked how have I coped with losing a daughter. I reply that we have been privileged to have met Steve soon after Lisa's passing, and because of that we have been given a greater understanding of what our life is for. In the beginning, just after we received the news, I really felt that there just wasn't any point in carrying on, in spite of having a loving family around us. We had seen Lisa go through so much trauma in her quest to become a ballet dancer, with so many highs and lows, and when she died I kept on asking what is the point of it all? But I have never said, "Why me?", because, why not me? Also I have never said, "What if?", because you can go on for ever with 'what ifs' and it wouldn't alter anything. There are so many of us in the world and many are suffering greater hardships than we will ever experience. Our loss is just a small pebble in a beach of circumstances and is but one moment in time. Grief can make you feel very alone, but there will be many others going through exactly the same thing as you at that same moment. I say to those who are despairing in their grief, spare others a thought and send a prayer out for them as well as for yourself, to ask for strength and for help in the days to come.

This world can be a cruel place. Why do some people suffer so much with illness and disability? In many countries, life is of little value, and starvation, murder and torture are commonplace. It is heartbreaking to see the little children not having a chance in life just because they have been born into a place that is rife with starvation and disease. Again one can ask, what is the point of it all? Every one of us has a personal responsibility, as our actions affect those around us. I didn't blame God for Lisa's death, and I could not hold him responsible for our grief. It was caused by the negligence of man, not God. I have heard many people say when they are grieving for a loved one: why has God let this happen? With his power, why does he let so many die from starvation and disease, tiny babies that haven't had a chance in life, young children with their lives before them? Well, I believe that it is not God's fault but man alone who has lost sight of his responsibility towards his fellow man and is too fond of putting the blame on others when things go wrong.

When Lisa passed on, we searched and searched for many months for a glimmer of hope that Lisa really was still with us, even though we could now no longer see her or touch her. We visited many psychics for a one-to-one meeting, but this didn't really help us, as I strongly feel that some people, while they might have a gift, think that they are better than they really are and let their own thoughts take over and try to please you with a reading. There are no qualifications for being a good psychic and it is up to you to be discerning if you require a reading. For the people who aren't sure what the difference is between a psychic and a medium I will explain, with many thanks to our good friend Sue Reece, of Paignton Spiritualist church, for her help!

PSYCHIC means working soul to soul incarnate. In other words, a good psychic will glean plenty of information about you and your life, and also your past and a small amount of your future, from the aura or energy field that surrounds your incarnate (living) body. You can receive some very good readings this way, with some excellent information, but this does not connect you to the spirit world.

MEDIUMSHIP means working soul to soul discarnate, in other words, with someone who has passed to Spirit.

CLAIRVOYANT means clear seeing, when the medium receives 'mind pictures' from the communicator in the spirit world, from which information can be taken about the communicator (evidence).

CLAIRSENTIENT means clear sensing, when the communicator imparts information on feelings, aches and pains, illnesses, and can sense the general demeanour of a person.

CLAIRAUDIENT means clear hearing, when the medium can actually hear words being spoken or words can just enter their mind; this way dates, names and numbers are given.

CLAIRKNOWING is when the medium just opens their mouth and allows the words to tumble out (a real act of faith).

Most mediums work with a combination of some or all of the above. Steve is clairaudient but also clairsentient, as he often feels people's pain when giving messages.

The aim of a good medium is to GIVE EVIDENCE OF SURVIVAL, giving proof to someone that their loved one lives on. They will communicate with someone from the spirit world, find the person in the audience with whom they wish to communicate and then give that person enough information about the communicator (discarnate soul) so that they have no doubt as to the identity of the communicator from the spirit world.

Roger and I now accept that Lisa will one day come through to us, but only when she is ready, and that she will probably do so in private as she did in the car to Steve on that particular evening. I have now learnt to say, "Thank you for letting me be her mother. It was a joy to have known her and I accept that she has returned to her real home and that we will meet again one day."

Our journey over the last fifteen years has been amazing, and I hope in writing this book that it will give those who are grieving the loss of a loved one a glimmer of hope. I now live in peace with the thought that our life has a definite purpose; long gone are the days when I had thought of giving up. We all have our path to travel along, which has been laid out for us, but at the end we will all go back to our real home and on that day we will meet our loved ones again. As for me, my epitaph will now read:

GONE HOME

SEE YOU ALL LATER!

EPILOGUE

The Last Fifteen Years - by Roger

When Lisa died, the world fell apart - or it seemed to at the time. I (we) felt so alone and helpless, and wanted to stop the world and tell it that our lovely Lisa had gone. Looking back to that awful day, and comparing it with now, I feel that I personally have developed a tremendous amount. Just as it is a privilege to know Steve (and to have met him so soon after Lisa's death), it was also a privilege to have known Lisa. She was vibrant, talented, passionate about her work and good fun; she loved life, shared my sense of humour and, above all, she was caring. In fact, at times she was the younger sister that I never had.

When we moved to the south-west in 1995, I was talking with a good friend one day - she was a healer, and very 'spiritual' - and she said to me, "Of course, you're down here for a reason you know." I replied, "Do you really think so?" She was adamant that we were. Well, after all the 'coincidences', and the path that our lives have taken - I am very happy to believe that now.

When I think back to the time that we asked Steve if he would come down here, I must admit that I did think to myself (as Jill did), "Well, if we can help the people down here in some small way, through seeing Stephen's wonderful gift, we have at least been able to help show them that all is not lost, when they may feel that it is."

It seems that our unseen friends and family know more about our lives here than we realise.

I know how some people will be feeling, when they watch Steve for the first time - just as we did fifteen years ago in Yorkshire!

I would like to think that I (and of course, we) have made a difference to peoples' lives - and that will be a suitable epitaph for me!